# HOW I SOLD 80,000 BOOKS

# BOOKS

## Book Marketing for Authors

**(Self Publishing through Amazon and Other Retailers)**
**Updated 2017 Edition**

by

**Multi-Award Winning,**
**#1 International Best-Selling Author**

# Alinka Rutkowska

# TABLE OF CONTENTS

Edited by Andrew Whiteside

ISBN: 978-1-943386-05-5

# DISCLAIMER

While every effort has been made to give an accurate representation of how to maximize your book sales, there is no guarantee that you will earn any money. Any product that tells you otherwise is misleading. Even though this industry is one of the few in which incredible earnings potential can be realized, there is never any guarantee.

Examples and income projections in this book are not to be interpreted as a promise or guarantee of earnings. Earnings potential is entirely dependent on the person utilizing the training programs, strategies, tools and resources.

# FREE VIDEO TRAINING

Get the step-by-step system I use to sell
books by the truckload: authorremake.com

Go to authorremake.com — I'll see you on the
inside!

# EDITORIAL REVIEWS

*A Fantastic Resource.*
*If only I had started with Alinka Rutkowska's* How I Sold 80,000 Books. *There's no fluff here, just clear, concise steps one can take to successfully market a book. Probably the best and most comprehensive one-stop guide I have seen, it provides a clear path for authors, agents and publishers alike. There are several pillars which support marketing success, the primary one being, as Alinka properly states, the product. The book world is awash with the dregs of poorly written works. So, how do you separate your crystalline work of literature from the rest? I would begin by reading* How I Sold 80,000 Books.

Rick DeStefanis
Award-Winning Author of The Gomorrah Principle
www.rickdestefanis.com

\*\*\*


*Alinka Rutkowska provides a wealth of information in* How I Sold 80,000 Books. *Whether you're a seasoned author or just starting out, there are plenty of tips that are sure to be helpful. Clear details and direction are provided along with links to various resources. I had the privilege of meeting Alinka through the Readers' Favorite forum. She is extremely knowledgeable and always willing to help authors in whatever way she can. I highly recommend this little gem of a book!*

Patti Tingen
Award-Winning Inspirational Author
www.pattitingenauthor.com

\*\*\*

*The must have resource for every author struggling with how to promote their book.* How I Sold 80,000 Books *by Alinka Rutkowska covers it all from web page to social media to promotion, sales and everything in between.*
*Do you know how to get reviews from Amazon Top Reviewers? It's in* How I Sold 80,000 Books *by Alinka Rutkowska. Need a list of top book award contests? You will find that in* How I Sold 80,000 Books *by Alinka Rutkowska.*
*If you are a new author or if you have published 100 books, you will find suggestions and tips in* How I Sold 80,000 Books *that is sure to help you reach your goals.*

Mary Adair
Award-Winning Author of Native American romance novels
www.maryadair.com

\*\*\*

*Alinka Rutkowska's* How I Sold 80,000 Books *is a 'must have' for all new and seasoned authors. This step-by-step guide gives straightforward, tried and tested methods, with detailed advice on how to avoid those bumps in the road that every writer encounters on their journey to becoming a best-selling author.*

*It covers everything from the moment you decide to write your novel to getting your work noticed by readers, including the editing process, formatting and book covers, getting your book in digital and printed format, reviews and awards, and most importantly, how to promote your work. She details the workings of social networks such as Facebook and Twitter, giving a comprehensive explanation of how to use them to your advantage.*

*Unlike most 'how to' books I have read in the past, Alinka presents the information in an easy-to-understand, friendly manner that makes you feel as if you are talking directly to the author. Although Alinka primarily writes children's books, she is also a coach for budding authors, and the information put forth can be applied to any genre, aiding all authors, even those who have taken a more traditional route with a large publishing house.*

*The links included in the book are like gold dust, and you will find yourself watching/ reading them over and over again as you forge your way through the publishing world. There are also direct links to sites such as Readers' Favorite and book blogs, which will save you hours of Internet trawling time, allowing you to spend more time doing the thing you love — writing your best-selling novel.*

*Publishing is a ruthless market where your work is quickly swallowed up in the masses of books released each year. Alinka demonstrates a path that prevents your work becoming invisible and forces it out into the limelight. Any author who wishes for their book to be seen should read Alinka's* How I Sold 80,000 Books *and follow the advice inside. I promise you, it will not steer you wrong, and I only wish that I'd had access to this when I first started out. It would have saved me months of work.*

Lyneal Jenkins
International Award-Winning, Best-Selling Author
http://lynealjenkins.com/

# SELECTED AMAZON REVIEWS

*Amazingly astute! Very informative, tells you right where to go and who to see to get your books sold.* Christi J. Hubbard

*This book is excellent. Packed with great information which can be put to use immediately. In fact, there's so much useful information, it will take me a while to implement it.* Judi Moreo

*I spent days to try to understand how to market and promote my first book, until I found* How I Sold 80,000 Books. Lilly B.

*This book offers some really great tips for new or seasoned authors. I can't wait to implement some of these practices in my book business. Warning though...it is A LOT to take in! :)* Becky W.

*This book was very informative. Gave terrific ideas on how to market a book - both ebooks and paper books. Highly recommended.* Neil Greenbaum

*This is a great book. It's full of useful information. I highly recommend it.* Jerry Minchey

*Very detailed and in-depth as I am walked through the 4Ps of self-publishing. Easy to understand and follow and even better, her methods are doable.* YedteD

*The best book for self-published writers I've read.* Desiree Tamargo

*Great resource for anyone looking to self-publish. Alinka gives you a lot of resources, from her experience and beyond. Great read for authors looking to publish anytime soon.* RJB

*I'm in the process of self-publishing a second novel, and I found* How I Sold 80,000 Books *really informative, clear, witty and full of concise realistic information. I loved the clarity of Alinka Rutkowska's book, with its relevant links to sites and extra information throughout.* Amanda Atkins

*The author provides sound advice. What I like most about this book (unlike so many other books on this subject) is that it is not filled with rehashed strategies and marketing tactics that don't work.* SouthernLadyWriter

*This book is awesome. It is a budding author's treasure. Practical and useable material. I highly recommend it.* Sheldon D. Newton

*This is a good, comprehensive resource on book marketing for authors. This should be on your "must read" list if you have or are considering publishing a book. Rutkowska's no-nonsense, step-by-step approach will set you on the path toward success as an author. I highly recommend this as a resource and will certainly keep it as a reference in the days ahead.* Author of *LYCCYX*

*There is a lot of good information in this book. It is easy to read and understand. For a beginning author it is a treasure trove of information.* Valerie Lull, author of *Ten Healthy Teas*

*The best reference for online book marketing. It provides information that is missing in similar publications.* argyle4087

*Amazing Marketing Tool. I was amazed at all the marketing tools in this quick read. There are things in there I don't think I would have ever considered. Now it's time to put them into action.* Tracy Pink

*The writer is more than an author. She is an entrepreneur. She looks at the business of self-publishing. Coming from that perspective she gives advice based on an author wanting to become a professional not just an indie author. There is a difference. The principles she teaches are timeless and make good business sense. This is the book you should read and follow but don't want to because it is work. Let's be honest success takes work. The advice she gives would and could change an author's success rates. Implement and see success.* Ericka K Thompson

*What I loved best about 80K Books is the straightforward discussion of setting up your book for success. The author provides exactly what she does to earn thousands of orders of her own books. The plan is one that can easily be implemented for authors of any genre. I appreciated the ease of applying the information - there was not a lot of filler to sift through, which made it easy to grab what I needed and get back to promoting my own books. Highly recommended - easily one of my favorite books on Kindle promotion.* Suzanne

*This book is a handy little guide for all authors. The author shares her own experiences with methods she used herself to get her own work noticed. The book is written as though the author speaks to us personally, with a friendly and personable voice. Her information is invaluable, and her strategies for marketing are right on the mark. I'd suggest every author who is looking for some good marketing ideas to take advantage of this book and keep it for a handy reference guide.* D.G. Kaye

*Great information. Wish I'd had this before my first published novel.* Drafty Spots

*The author gave significant insights into a multiple ways to help authors sell more books. Her real-life examples and personal insights were understandable and can easily be placed into action.* Keith D. Maderer

*Glad I took the time to read and underline this book. Lots of good ideas and advice for authors of fiction too.* N. Goodman

*Often when I see this type of title, I am skeptical on whether the information contained inside will actually be beneficial. I have to say this was. Although the book just gave hints of things in the beginning, the author slowly built her case and method for book creation, crafting, promotion, reviews and more. She kept giving and I must give her 5 stars! Thanks for putting this together and making it available!* Live Laugh Love

*I definitely appreciate publishing advice from a SUCCESSFUL author! This book is a gem and I wish I'd read it last year. I'm re-reading it right now, as we speak:)* karidsg

*I think the book is brilliant. The book may be short (relatively speaking) but it is Jam-packed with practical ideas to promote your book and increase your sales. Author is practically giving*

*away book selling secrets for free! Must-read for all authors - new, established, and especially those going the self-published route.* Anupama

# ABOUT THE AUTHOR

Alinka Rutkowska is multi-award-winning and #1 international best-selling author. She's a coach who transforms struggling writers into profitable authorpreneurs.

She's the founder and CEO of LibraryBub, which connects librarians with award-winning and best-selling books from independent publishers.

She's the founder and host of the "5-Figure Author Challenge," which gives authors winning strategies to get to 5 figures in 5 months.

She's been featured on Fox Business Network, affiliates of ABC and NBC, Author Marketing

Club, The Author Hangout, Kindlepreneur, Book Marketing Mentors, Examiner, She Knows, She Writes, The Writer's Life and many more.

She's been voted top 5 speaker and named most creative book marketer at the Bestseller Summit Online.

Alinka is passionate about helping authors succeed, that's why she created a free video training which reveals the step-by-step system she uses to sell books by the truckload.

Sign up now to replicate her success: authorremake.com

# INTRODUCTION

Writing is my passion, marketing is my vocation. Blending the two together is what I believe allowed me to sell 80,000+ copies of my books.

Let me answer two burning questions I often get from fellow authors. Yes, I really did sell over 80,000 copies of my titles and no, it did not happen overnight and it did not all happen via Amazon. This number includes online sales, special bulk sales and sales of foreign rights. There are different avenues to achieving what you want.

I have tried and failed many times but I've never given up. I keep learning and testing and after five years in the publishing business I've figured out what works, at least what works for me, but I believe that it will work for you too.

Everyone's path to success is different. Even everyone's definition of success is different. But marketing your book and optimizing it for success starts even before you start writing your book. It's difficult to look at it this way at the beginning but after having published 20+ titles I am now able to see clearly that there are four elements (four Ps) that determine your book's success.

If you've studied marketing, you will already know what these Ps stand for. In this book I go through each of them in great detail to show you how I optimize my books for success and how you can do it too.

Some issues are covered in only one sentence - that's because I cut out all the fluff that increases word count. It's important that you give those issues just as much attention as you give those that I write more extensively about.

It would be beneficial if you read this book multiple times and definitely each time before you publish a new title.

Even if you know about everything I cover (which is possible for veteran authors), I'm sure you will appreciate a reminder. I certainly read this book (which I've written myself!) before publishing new titles, simply because sometimes we forget.

# THE 4 PS NECESSARY TO SELL THOUSANDS OF BOOKS

So you've published a book and now you're ready to market it? I have good news and bad news. Which do you want to hear first? O.K., I'll decide. The bad news is that it's already too late to start marketing your title. The good news is that we'll make the most of what we have and get you geared for success.

What does it even mean to market a book? If you attend a Marketing 101 lecture at any university, you'll see that the professor's first PowerPoint slide will prominently display the "Marketing Mix", which consists of four Ps (and I don't mean the green stuff you're sometimes served on your plate).

The professor will announce that the four Ps stand for Product, Place, Price and Promotion. The students will yawn, text, doodle or maybe even take notes.

# PRODUCT

Your book is your product, thus the most important part of your marketing mix. For teaching purposes, let's dissect your product (not because it's dead, because we will resurrect it) to its core, its add-ons and its metadata.

## YOUR PRODUCT'S CORE

You know that your book is amazing, that it's the best it can ever be and that it's award-winning material, right? "How am I supposed to know?" you'll say. "I'll know that when I put it on the market and submit it for some awards." Not exactly.

As Ernest Hemingway is said to have elegantly put it, "The first draft of anything is shit."

### EDITING

Of course YOU'VE revised your manuscript countless times, and you've had it professionally edited and proofread. I take it for granted.

When I say "professionally edited", I don't mean that your high school classmate who was good at English did it for you. Go online and look for editors, contact your high school teachers and find out if they also do this for a living or, for goodness sake, ask your hairdresser if he knows of a proofreader. Hairdressers usually know everyone!

Remember that there are three types of editors:

1) developmental editor who can tell you that your story will make great wrapping paper unless you get it significantly revised;
2) copy editor who will make you feel like you didn't do your homework as he points out all your errors;
3) proofreader who will read your masterpiece countless times and make sure it's at its purest state possible.

If you're producing a great product, you need all three.

## CRITIQUE GROUPS

But how do you know that what you are submitting to your editor is quality material? The answer is: a critique group. A critique group is a very peculiar animal. It's not a circle of mutual adoration as you will find in many first-time author groups swapping reviews. It's not a place for the author to be worshipped by loving kin. A critique group consists of a group of writers who regularly critique their manuscripts. They write in the same genre, they know their craft and they both provide and receive critiques.

I belong to a group like this. We are five writers, most of whom are not yet published but really know their writing. Every month we swap manuscripts. I critique four different stories, and I receive four different critiques of my manuscript. There are some guidelines to critiquing that we use. For example, I usually don't say, "This is crap, flush it down the toilet." Instead I comment, "Have you considered eliminating this character/part as I think it doesn't move the story forward?" I know they do the same for me.

## WRITING COURSES

How do you find a critique group? I think that the best way is to take an offline or online course on writing as critique groups are pretty much a natural thing happening there, somewhat like green grass growing after a bountiful rain.

"I'm an author! Why should I take a course in writing?" you might say. Well, even if you have a PhD in bestseller writing, things change all the time. Readers want different things, publishers take notice and agents then solicit that type of stuff. Even if you don't care about traditional publishing, you still want your books to compete with the best, don't you?

I aim at taking one new writing course each year. This is very helpful, particularly if you want to change genres.

One thing I want to say to children's authors, and those considering writing a children's book, please take a course. It only seems easy. And for those attempting to write in rhyme, if you don't know what rhythm and meter are, please don't torture your readers with:

"This book is the best you will ever read,
and I know it for sure,
I know it indeed.
How do I know it?
Some readers may ask,
You'll soon find out,
it will be an easy task..."

I know it rhymes, but it sucks.

## YOUR PRODUCT'S ADD-ONS

Let's now assume that the core of your product is flawless. You've had it critiqued and you've reviewed it countless times, you've had it proofread several times, you've read it over 20 times yourself and you can't even look at it any longer. Let's move on to your product's add-ons.

## COVER

This is so obvious that I don't even want to spend time discussing it. Your cover must be created by a professional. Forget those pre-made templates, they won't make you stand out anywhere: not with the readers, not with reviewers, and not with boards of judges deciding who the next award will go to.

Resize it to a thumbnail and see what it looks like. If you can't read the title or understand what's on the cover, neither will your readers who will view your books online as thumbnails.

No, you don't have to spend a fortune to get a professional cover. One of the many places you can go to is Fiverr (https://www.fiverr.com) where freelancers can get you a cover for as little as $5 (you will probably need to pay a little more than that but with $20 you can have a fantastic cover). I used a Fiverr freelancer to create the cover for this book.

## FORMATTING

This is another super obvious thing, but I must mention it: make sure your text has been professionally formatted so that it looks great.

This is especially important for picture books. And talking about picture books you will be safest if you hire a graphic designer. If you want to hook the little ones, you need to provide exceptional content.

## EMAIL MARKETING

I know we're only at the first P, but it's not part of the marketing mix for nothing. Your book is the primary place where you will insert a link to your website, telling readers that they can get some awesome free goodies if they go to your URL. When they go there, they will need to provide their email in exchange for a free digital download and you will start building your list of loyal fans. We'll get back to this in the Promotion section.

## REQUEST FOR REVIEW

We know that reviews can make or break a book, but even more important than the quality of reviews is its quantity (no, no typo here). At the end of your book insert a request to leave a review online. Don't beg. Simply tell the reader how happy it would make you. I do this in the form of a funny limerick (not as crappy as my poem in the Writing Courses section).

Another idea, incorporate a request for review in your autoresponder sequence. If someone subscribes to your mailing list, they are quite committed already. They are your best readers and they will often happily leave a review, if you remind them.

## FEATURING OTHER BOOKS

If you've published other books or you will have new books coming out shortly, make sure to list them prominently inside your book or on the back cover.

You might also want to partner with other authors in your genre and feature their books at the back of yours. They would do the same thing for you and this way you will drive readers to one another.

## BIO

People want to know who their new favorite author is, so insert an interesting bio. Nobody cares when you graduated or what your favorite pizza topping is. Make it short and meaningful but funny. Here's one of the bios I use:

*Alinka Rutkowska lives in a castle with her family and dragon just like Cinderella and writes picture books for children like you.*

*She has written more than 20 books, and she has received many awards for her work. She is the winner of the prestigious International Readers' Favorite Book Award Contest, and her book series received the acclaimed Mom's Choice Award.*

Short and memorable.

## PICTURE

You need a professional picture so go get it done and make sure it's your best shot because you will use it on your book covers, website, brochures, business cards and all social media networks.

Keep it consistent. People will recognize you by your avatar so make sure you have the same picture EVERYWHERE.

## YOUR PRODUCT'S METADATA

Metadata is all the stuff that makes your book easy to find for those hungry, hungry readers. Let's talk about the title, subtitle, keywords and description.

### TITLE

Your title is key. It has to grab your readers' attention just like the cover. It has to be short, sweet and powerful, and full of key words. That's not an easy task. Luckily if you look around, you'll find software that helps identify the words used in best-selling titles!

## SUBTITLE

This is where you want to use keywords to make your book easy to search for. But what keywords should you use? Amazon itself provides you with a great tool! Just go to the Amazon search box on the top of the page and start typing anything. Amazon will give you suggestions, which is what your readers are looking for! This is also the stuff you need to put in your subtitle!

## KEYWORDS

Why bother with keywords? Because Amazon and other online retailers may look like bookstores but in reality, they're search engines and it's through keywords that readers find your books!

A good place to start is the Amazon search box which can help you identify the keywords that might work. The problem with this approach is that it can take hours or days and you will still end up guessing what the best keywords are.

But have no fear. I have you covered. There are tools that are so much better. I explain them in detail at authorremake.com.

As soon as I optimized the keywords for one of my books its sales multiplied by a factor of 50 (I kid you not).

## DESCRIPTION

This is one of the most important components that your readers will look at when making the decision as to whether to buy your book. I love to start my description with an editorial review from Readers' Favorite at https://readersfavorite.com/book-reviews.htm. The great thing about this organization is that you can submit your book for review before it's published, and you can have an editorial review to display on launch day!

This is how you incorporate it in your Amazon description:

Go to your Author Central account.
Click on Books.
Click on the title of the book.
The first tab you'll see is Editorial Reviews.
Go to Review or Product Description and paste your review(s) there!

Now they will appear on your book's Amazon page!

Ninja tip: make sure to insert some of your keywords into your description!

## PAPER BOOK OR EBOOK?

I really don't understand this question. Why would one have to choose or limit themselves to just one if it's so easy to create both.

Some people will never adapt to new technology and want paper. Others fully embrace new technology and read on their kindles, iPads, nooks and other devices. Still others might want your book in various formats, so make sure your give them a wide selection, including audio.

## SERIES

Once you've found initial success with your first release, consider making it a series. A series tends to sell well. We will talk more about this in the Promotion section.

If you know that your product is of top-notch quality, we can now move forward to the next P.

# PLACE

Now that we've got your product covered, let's move to WHERE you're going to sell it. "EVERYWHERE!" I hear you say, "Yeah, me too. Even *Harry Potter* isn't everywhere."

First of all, let's divide this 'place' thing into two separate worlds: online and offline. If you're reading this book, you know what "online" means — this alone makes you pretty technologically advanced. I'm only comparing you to my Italian mother-in-law who still doesn't know the difference between the computer and the Internet. She does, however, love books and they are one of her favorite impulse purchases at the gas station, supermarket or airport and right after spaghetti.

## ONLINE

If you are publishing your book independently, this will be your first, and initially, main point of sale. Saying, "I sell my book online", however, is somewhat similar to saying, "I like food". It's not very precise.

While offline you will obviously sell your paper books, online you can sell both and often on the same platform.

## AMAZON

An article in the *Wire* in May 2014 stated that "Amazon has basically no competition among online booksellers". So this is really where you need to start and what you need to care about most.

There are different ways of getting on Amazon. There is the print-on-demand (POD) way, which is easiest with CreateSpace, a company that belongs to Amazon. If you publish with CreateSpace, one of its prime features is easy access to Amazon. And since it's print-on-demand, you don't have to worry about inventory, shipping or anything. All you need to do is market your book and when somebody buys on Amazon, CreateSpace will print it and ship it. Your book will never be out of stock, and it's completely hassle free.

The downside to print-on-demand is that the production cost per unit is higher than if you went with a printer and printed 3,000 books. But then where would you keep them? And would you be packaging each book and running to the post office to send them? If this is the path for you then you would want to use something called Amazon Advantage (https://www.amazon.com/gp/seller-account/mm-product-page.html?topic=200329780).

There are instances when going with a printer is the better choice, the most obvious is if you want a certain quality that you can't get with POD and if you have a big offline order to fulfill.

## KINDLE DIRECT PUBLISHING (KDP)

According to a late 2013 *Forbes* article, Kindle is the most popular device for ebooks, beating even the Apple iPad. So right after you get your paper book on Amazon, run to KDP at https://kdp.amazon.com and get yourself an ebook version. Here are some tools and resources you can use to convert your book into an electronic version: https://kdp.amazon.com/help?topicId=A3IWA2TQYMZ5J6.

For my children's books I use the first on the list, Kindle Kids' Book Creator, which is very easy to navigate.

The great thing about KDP is that now you can schedule your launch day and sell copies prior to release date, which will boost your ranking on day one! (Unfortunately not all of these pre-orders will contribute to your launch-day ranking but it's still a great way to attract attention to your book).

## BARNES & NOBLE

Barnes & Noble is the next place to be. I didn't do anything in particular to have all of my books there, except for switching on one of the channels in my CreateSpace dashboard, but here's a great page that will answer all your questions on how to get your book into Barnes & Noble: http://www.barnesandnoble.com/help/cds2.asp?pid=8153

### NOOK

Just like Amazon has its Kindle, Barnes & Noble has its NOOK. Go to NOOK Press to publish your ebook directly to Barnes & Noble's ebook platform: https://www.nookpress.com/ebooks

According to the site itself, *NOOK Press gives you everything you need to create, edit, and sell your digital books through the NOOK Bookstore all in one place. It's easy to sign up and try out the features, such as writing, editing, formatting and collaborating. Then when you're ready to publish, simply fill out the vendor information and Submit. Once you're approved as a NOOK Press Vendor, your NOOK Books are ready to be sold at NOOK, and you'll be able to track your sales and payment information on your Sales page.*

### APPLE

Apple's iBooks is the second largest ebook market player right after Amazon's Kindle. To create a book for iBooks go to iBooks Author at https://www.apple.com/ibooks-author/ and drag and drop your text into a beautiful publication. The downside with this is that the book you create with this software is completely stand-alone, and you can't convert it for use on any other platform.

You can publish your book to the Apple store directly from iBooks Author and then you can manage your sales in iTunes Connect at https://itunesconnect.apple.com

Or, download iTunes Producer (under Book Delivery at https://itunesconnect.apple.com/WebObjects/iTunesConnect.woa/ra/ng/resources page) and use it to upload a ready ePub file.

### KOBO

The next stop in publishing your book is Kobo at http://www.kobo.com/writinglife. In August 2013, Kobo was the second largest ebook retailer in Japan, and *Forbes* estimated it at three percent of the market share in the United States.

### AGGREGATORS

You can upload your ebook to all the various platforms independently and retain all your royalties (except for the platform fees/percentages each company takes) or you can use Smashwords (http://www.smashwords.com), which is the world's largest distributor of indie ebooks.

An alternative to Smashwords is Draft2Digital (https://www.draft2digital.com), which, according to the site itself, is a *single, easy-to-use portal where you can convert your manuscript into an expertly-formatted ebook and publish it through some of the industry's most powerful retailers.*

### YOUR WEBSITE

All these different platforms are great and the more presence you have, the more potential readers you can reach. Once you've established a fan base of your own, however, (and a mailing list, which we will talk about in the Promotion section) the best way for both you and your fans is to sell your ebook directly from your website. I do this by creating special super-savings packs and selling them for much less than the online retailers. I retain the same royalty, but you can structure this any way you want.

Technologically speaking, all you need is a PayPal button and once your reader pays you,

you can email them their copy. And if you're a little more technologically advanced, you can create a membership site, so once your reader makes the purchase, they'll be redirected to a secure area from where they can download your book(s), and you can be having spaghetti bolognese with a nice glass of Barolo wine, not having to worry about a thing!

I created my website and membership site with OptimizePress (http://alinkarutkowska.com/optimizepress) and I heartily recommend it

## OFFLINE

So how can my mother-in-law access my book if she doesn't know the difference between the computer and the Internet? Offline.

## MAJOR BOOKSTORES, SCHOOLS & LIBRARIES

In order to get your book into major bookstores and libraries, it needs to be available via Ingram (http://www.ingramcontent.com) or Baker & Taylor (http://www.baker-taylor.com). CreateSpace does open this door for you, but there are so many middlemen that bookstores don't want to purchase self-published books because it's too expensive for them. Plus there's the issue of them not being able to return the books.

Ingram works with independently published authors via Ingram Spark (https:// www1.ingramspark.com). As they state on their website, *world literary domination may not have been your goal but with access to over 39,000 booksellers, online retailers, and libraries around the world, IngramSpark is the missing link.* Also *IngramSpark connects your book to every single major ebook retailer in the world; the big boys like Amazon Kindle, iBooks, and Kobo as well as 70 emerging ebook retailers.*

For a comparison between CreateSpace and IngramSpark go here: http:// www.selfpublishingadvice.org/watchdog- ingram-spark-vs-createspace-for-self- publishing-print-books/

Baker & Taylor is the second largest U.S. book wholesaler. According to Aaron Shepard at http://www.newselfpublishing.com/ CreateSpaceEDC.html *the truth is, B&T sells to bookstores as well as to schools and libraries, just as Ingram sells to schools and libraries as well as to bookstores. But each wholesaler has its area of primary strength.*

Baker & Taylor has its own POD service called TextStream (http://www.btol.com/ supplier textstream about.cfm? CFID=220725221&CFTOKEN=90331476) According to its site *leveraging TextStream alongside Baker & Taylor's unsurpassed network of more than 40,000 customers worldwide is a winning formula. As a TextStream client, your titles and all supporting data are sent to thousands of Internet retailers, bookstores, mass marketers, schools, libraries and universities.*

Some authors choose to publish both with CreateSpace (to have easy access to Amazon) and with Ingram Spark (to reach offline retailers). The best way to do this is to buy your own ISBN via Bowker at https://www.myidentifiers.com and use the same one with both platforms.

## LIBRARYBUB

Having your book available in the library catalogues is like having your book on Amazon. It's the primary avenue of getting your book into the hands of librarians, or readers in the case of Amazon.

But neither Amazon nor Baker & Taylor or Ingram will actively promote your book, especially if you're an indie author.

That's why I created LibraryBub - the only service on the market that connects indie authors with over 10,000 libraries.

If you have an award-winning, best-selling or positively reviewed book (by Kirkus, Readers' Favorite or similar), apply for feature at http://librarybub.com/authors/.

## SUPERMARKETS

Supermarkets stock mostly paperback fiction, and children's books sell well as do cookbooks and titles by regional authors. According to Brian Jud at http://www.bookmarketingworks.com/SelltoAirports.htm *if you can demonstrate that your promotional activities will help bring in new customers and profits, you will get their attention. You may submit your book and marketing package directly to the major supermarket chains, but they normally direct you to their wholesalers.*

## AIRPORTS

The sky's the limit.

According to Brian Jud at http://www.bookmarketingworks.com/SelltoAirports.htm *bookstores in most small airports have space constraints limiting the titles they*
*stock to only the top fiction and nonfiction titles as well as the popular classics. But a title does not have to be a bestseller to find its way into the stores in large airports. These shops will*

*carry titles by local and regional authors, as well as books pertaining to its specific locale and destination points. For example, the title* Fenway: A Biography in Words and Pictures, *by Dan Shaughnessy and Stan Grossfeld, can be found in bookstores in Boston's Logan Airport.*

*Titles for children tend to do well in these outlets, as do titles for business travelers who spend a good amount of time in airports. Also titles on management, investment, economics, business biography, personal finance and health work well in the airport setting.*

You need to submit your book directly to the airport bookstore chains.

## CRUISE LINES

They say the sky's the limit — but what about the sea? I'm selling my children's book series on numerous cruise ships and when they order we are no longer talking about a couple of copies. Their trial order was 800 copies and the subsequent ones run by the thousands. It's a little tricky to get in though. Your book needs to be somewhat linked to the sea. You need to get in touch with the retail department and try to attract their attention. I find LinkedIn is a great platform to look for professionals in the retail department who you'd like to contact to negotiate your book sales with.

## INDEPENDENT BOOKSTORES / GIFT SHOPS

These are great since they make decisions by themselves, and you can often talk to the decision maker as soon as you enter the store. Here's what I suggest you do:

1) Get in a bookstore/gift shop that is thematically linked with your book.

2) Browse and make sure to take a look at the books section (or your genre).

3) When you see a shop assistant that's not busy, approach her with your book in your hand and say: "Hi, I'm an author and I wrote a book about xxx. I was wondering if you'd be interested in carrying it in your store (next season)?"

4) They will most likely reply: "It's my manager who takes care of this and she'll be back tomorrow."

5) Say: "OK, can I leave you a brochure? This is the book I'm talking about. It just received a [name award or honor or best-selling status - or something else that makes it special] and I'm also selling it in [name where - Amazon is also good to name.]"

6) Get a subscriber on your list! I say: "Do you have small children in your family? Nephews? Nieces? Friends with children?" I give them my card and say: "Go to my website, enter your email and I'll send you one of my books for free."

They are then super happy and will certainly pass your info to the manager.

7) Then say: "Oh, can you please give me an email that I can follow up with?" They give you the manager's email and a couple of days later you send an email pitching your book.

If you get to talk to the manager (always negotiate with the decision maker), they will ask you about your retail price, the price you give her (industry standard is 55 to 60 percent discount off the retail price - negotiate that), she will ask you where you ship from because she will be paying for freight.

And here you are - the start of a long-term business relationship and increased visibility for your books!

## GAS STATIONS, THERAPIST OFFICES, ETC...

You can get your book basically anywhere. The key is to THINK THEMES. Is your book about curing an illness? Talk to hospitals about getting it in their gift shops! Is your book about fish? Talk to aquariums and get your book in their gift shops! Is your book about cruise ships? You know where I'm going with this...

Make sure you find the decision maker—be professional and polite and get your book in those gift stores around the world!

## YOUR WEBSITE

Last but not least you can sell your paper book directly from your website. All you need is a PayPal button, and you'll get your buyer's payment and shipping address. You'll wrap the book, go to the post office and you're done! Or you can send your book directly through your POD dashboard without the need to handle the inventory, packaging and shipping. Easy!

Direct sales are always your most lucrative ones because you get rid of the middleman.

# PRICE

In other words: How much?!

Again we need to divide this into two categories: physical books and ebooks.

## PHYSICAL BOOKS

The first thing you need to do is research your competition, see what they charge and be competitive. You also need to make sure that you will be making money.

Another thing you need to consider, if you will be selling to any of the physical entities we covered in the Place section, is that you need to be able to give them a standard industry discount which is 55 to 60 percent off the list price and still be profitable.

If you've secured a big order (see the cruise ship example), your best choice here would be to go with a printer instead of POD, that's because you can be both more competitive against other similar titles and your margin will be higher, which means more spaghetti and wine for everyone!

## EBOOKS

Ebooks are different because there is no printing cost, no inventory, no shipping, no fees, maybe except for download fees.

Readers expect an ebook to cost $9.99 or less, or they won't consider buying it. The standard tends to be between $0.99 and $4.99 — I know what you're thinking but that's just the way it is.

Again you need to research your competition and test your price point to get it right.

## SERIES

The great thing about a series is that you can make the first book permanently free (permafree) and hook the reader to get them to buy the subsequent books for a regular price.

You can't publish a permanently free book via KDP but you can be sneaky and do the following: publish your book on Kindle for $0.99 and everywhere else (iTunes, Kobo, NOOK) for free. Then contact KDP support and ask them to price-match.

As soon as they do it, you will have a permafree book which will be your business card.

Free books get 50 times more downloads than $0.99 books and with one free book you can give incredible exposure to all your other titles.

It's sort of like the free cheese samples you get in supermarkets. You would never have found that particular cheese if they hadn't offered it to you for free but once you've tasted it you go back to buy it again and again and again!

If for some reason you want to start charging for your permafree book (because you added a lot of content, got hundreds of reviews or have a different permafree book), all you need to do is contact KDP support again and ask them to price match with other platforms who are now carrying your title at a higher price point (so, again, start with the other platforms).

### KDP SELECT

Once your book is on KDP (see the Place section), you can decide whether you want to enroll your book in KDP Select. According to the website (https://kdp.amazon.com/select?language=en US) joining the program allows you to:

4) *Earn higher royalties (Earn your share of the KDP Select Global Fund amount when readers choose and read more than 10 percent of your book from Kindle Unlimited, or borrow your book from the Kindle Owners' Lending Library. Plus, earn 70 percent royalty for sales to customers in Japan, India, Brazil and Mexico.)*

5)  *Maximize your book's sales potential (Choose between two great promotional tools: Kindle Countdown Deals, time-bound promotional discounting for your book while earning royalties; or Free Book Promotion where readers worldwide can get your book free for a limited time.)*

6)  *Reach a new audience (Help readers discover your books by making them available through Kindle Unlimited in the U.S, U.K., Germany, Italy, Spain, France and Brazil and the Kindle Owners' Lending Library (KOLL) in the U.S, U.K., Germany, France, and Japan).*

Sounds too good to be true? That's probably because it is! As the good people at KDP warn: *When you choose to enroll your book in KDP Select, you're committing to make the digital format of that book available exclusively through KDP. During the period of exclusivity, you cannot distribute your book digitally anywhere else, including on your website, blogs, etc.*

So, as you see, it's a tradeoff. If you go for KDP Select, forget about distributing your book via NOOK, Apple, Kobo, Smashwords, your website, and basically anywhere else… at least during the 90-day period you're subscribing for. If, however, you do go for it, you can use promotional tools such as Free Kindle Days and Kindle Countdown which can significantly boost your Amazon sales.

I've recently noticed that the books I haven't enrolled into KDP Select are doing very well on other platforms and I will now be gradually pulling more of my titles out of Select. But it's a decision every author has to make for themselves. Both approaches can be lucrative if you know what you're doing.

And that's why you are reading this in the Price section — the Free Kindle Days, the Kindle Countdown Deal, and the permanently free book allow you to play with this important P.

# PROMOTION

"Is she done yet?" If this is what you're thinking, I have bad news. Not even close! Not only do you need to produce an amazing book, make important decisions about its distribution and price, you now have to promote it big time or it will just drown in the ever expanding ocean of books.

Instead of providing you with 100 random ideas for promoting your book, I'll go through those promotional activities that have been working well for me followed by a couple of things which I'll be adding to my mix shortly.

Again, we will divide this section into an online and offline part, but as I've hinted in the Product section, there are a few promotional tweaks you need to include inside your book first!

## WITHIN BOOK

### THAT AWARD STICKER

If you've won any book awards, you absolutely MUST advertise it on your book cover! My foreign rights agent told me that the books foreign publishers are most interested in are those with award stickers on their covers!

Here's a list of book award contests for 2017:

My absolute favorite: Readers' Favorite International Book Award Contest

Deadline **April 1, 2017** (late deadline is June 1).

You can win one of $35,000 in prizes just for entering and you get a chance to have your book made into a movie or TV show by Wind Dancer Films.

All winners get a free certificate, medals, stickers and digital seals. They also get displayed at the International Miami Book Fair free of charge and there are many more perks!
Fee:
$89 for Early Bird Registration (April 1);
$99 Regular Registration Deadline (May 1);
$109 Late Registration (June 1).

Of course there are many more book award contests but this is my absolute favorite! I participated in the previous years and I won. I went to the Miami Awards Ceremony, had an absolutely wonderful time and made invaluable connections with fellow authors, agents and business people.

And here's all the rest (you have to do your own due diligence before registering. I'm just listing these for you):

**January 15, 2017** Foreword Reviews (Foreword INDIES Book of the Year Awards): Publicity efforts will help readers discover fabulous books from the independent book industry. Foreword INDIES annually honors more than 250 winners in 66 categories. By entering your book into the awards program, you will automatically receive a year long subscription to the quarterly *Foreword Reviews.* Winners will be featured in the Fall issue of *Foreword Reviews.*

Fee: $99

**January 21, 2017** Eric Hofer Awards: Grand prize $2,000. Category winner, runner-up, and honorable mention(s), Montaigne Medal for most thought-provoking book(s), da Vinci Eye for superior book cover(s), First Horizon for debut author(s), Individual Press Awards for Micro, Small and Academic presses, as well as self-published books.
Fee: $55

**January 31, 2017** Beverly Hills Book Awards: The Beverly Hills Book Award™ judges recognize winning books that demonstrate a wide scope of criteria that makes for an excellent overall presentation.
Fee: $75

**February 10, 2017** Nautilus Awards Book Awards: Their core mission remains to celebrate and honor books that support conscious living, green values, high-level wellness and spiritual growth.
Fee: $185

**February 17, 2017** Next Generation Indie Book Awards: The top 70 books will be forwarded to a leading literary agent for review and possible presentation. Winners will receive an invitation to attend the Gala Awards Reception held at an outstanding location in Chicago during BEA and will also receive a cash prize, trophy and medals.
Fee: $75

**February 25, 2017** Independent Publisher Book Awards: Conducted annually, the Independent Publisher Book Awards honor the year's best independently published titles from around the world. Each announced book will receive a gold, silver or bronze medal, a personalized certificate, and 20 foil seal.

Entry fees range from the early bird fee of $75 to $95 when you enter closer to the final deadline. Regional and ebook category entries are $55 when added to a national category entry.

**March 1, 2017** (submissions open) SCBWI work-In-Progress Grant: You must be a current SCBWI member when your work is submitted and when the award is announced in September. You may not submit a work that is under contract. If the work becomes under contract before the award is announced, you will become ineligible. You may submit only one WIP grant category per year.

Your first year of membership in the SCBWI is $95. The annual renewal fee is $80.

**March 27, 2017** Parents' Choice Awards: The Parents' Choice Awards committees look for products that entertain and teach with flair, stimulate imagination and inspire creativity. Judges are interested in how a product helps a child grow in many ways: socially, intellectually, emotionally, ethically and physically. Products must be free of racial or gender bias. Above all, products must not extol violence.
Fee: $100

**March 31, 2017** The National Indie Excellence Book Awards: Winners and finalists can highlight their award on their marketing materials. They can download the seal to print on their books. Stickers will be available for purchase as well as certificates.
Fee: $75

**April 3, 2017** Writer's Digest Book Awards: Exact date has yet to be announced. Possibility to win $8,000 in cash; national exposure for your work; the attention of prospective editors and publishers; a paid trip to the ever-popular Writer's Digest Conference.
Fee: $99

**April 15, 2017** Literary Classics International Book Awards and Reviews: One gold and one silver award will be selected in each category for the International Book Award. Each book award honoree will receive an award certificate and 25 sample seals. Additional award seals will be made available for purchase.
Fee: $95

**April 25, 2017** San Francisco Book Festival: The grand prize for the 2016 San Francisco Book Festival winner is $1,500 cash appearance fee and a flight to San

Francisco for the gala awards ceremony in May 2016. Exact date TBD.
Fee: $75

**April 30, 2017** International Book Awards: As an honored winner or finalist you will have the right to highlight your award on your book cover, website, and marketing material. Award stickers will be available for purchase for all winners and finalists in each category.
Fee: $79

**May 1, 2017** Readers' Favorite International Book Award Contest: details above this list.
Fee:
$89 for Early Bird Registration (April 1);
$99 Regular Registration Deadline (May 1);
$109 Late Registration (June 1).

**May 1, 2017** Purple Dragonfly Book Awards: The Purple Dragonfly Book Awards are geared toward stories that appeal to children of all ages that inspire, inform, teach or entertain. A Purple Dragonfly Book Awards seal on your book's cover tells parents, grandparents, educators and caregivers they are giving children the very best in reading excellence.

Fee: $65

**May 25, 2017** New York Book Festival: The grand prize for the New York Book Festival Author of the Year is a $1,500 appearance fee and a flight to New York for the June awards.

Fee: $50

**May 31, 2017** The Indie Spiritual Book Awards: Category winner will receive a TISBA 2017 Category Winner, a virtual sticker, a one-minute book trailer and a listing in the Winners' Circle on the TISBA website. A review of each winning entry will be posted on the TISBA Review Blog.

Fee: $33.

**August 31, 2017** Best Indie Book Awards: Each winner will receive the Best Indie Book Award emblem to display on their website and book cover and winners will have their book featured on the sidebar of four websites for at least six months.

Fee: $50

**October 25, 2017 (TBC)** Cybils Awards, (Children's and Young Adult's Literary Awards).

**November 19, 2017 (TBC)** Illumination Awards: Contest for Christian books. Gold, silver and bronze medals will be awarded in each category. Each medal-winning book receives a packet including the medal, a certificate, 20 foil award seals, and awards marketing material.

Early-bird entry fee is $75 per title, per category until the first early-bird deadline, $85 during the second early-bird period, and then $95 until the final deadline.

**December 1, 2017 (TBC)** Readers' Views Literary Awards: Reader Views Literary Awards are open to all authors regardless of residency, however, the books must be published in the English language and targeted for the North American market.

Fee: $85 to $105

**December 31, 2017 (TBC)** Jane Addams Children's Book Awards: Given annually to the children's books published the preceding year that effectively promote the cause of peace, social justice, world community, and the equality of the sexes and all races as well as meeting conventional standards for excellence.

Fee: unknown

**December 31, 2017** USA Best Book Awards: No dates yet for 2017 submission, USA Book News covers books from all sections of the publishing industry — mainstream, independent and self-published.

Fee: $59

**Ongoing** Indie Reader's Discovery Awards: Prizes are: an IndieReader "All About the Book" feature, a sticker pronouncing your book an IndieReader Discovery Awards winner, an IRDA Winner designation in IndieReader's new app.
Fee: $150 per title, $ 50 additional entry

**Ongoing** The Mom's Choice Awards (MCA) evaluates products and services created for children, families and educators. The organization is based in the United States and has reviewed thousands of entries from more than 55 countries.

Fee: $500

**Ongoing** Story Monsters, fee $85 (Children's Literature)

**Ongoing** Creative Child Awards, fee $75 (Children's Literature)

Costa Book Awards No exact date yet for 2017 submission.

But what if you haven't received any awards yet? No problem, submit your book for a review at https://readersfavorite.com/book-reviews.htm and if you get a five star review, you can use that on your cover! What I do is get the Five Express Reviews Package because I like things to happen fast, and I maximize my chances of getting the sticker because only one review needs to be a five star for you to be able to use that badge!

Even better — submit your manuscript for review so that you can publish your first edition with a five star sticker on its cover! Readers love books that have been recognized by professional institutions, because they have proof that they are reading a high-quality product.

### LINK TO MAILING LIST

Your number one objective here is to get your current readers on your mailing list, so that you can sell them your subsequent books! The people who've bought from you once are the most likely to buy from you again!

So inside your book, you have to tell your readers to go and subscribe to your mailing list. But, of course, nobody will… unless you give them a good reason to do so. Offer them an irresistible product that will be waiting for them right after they subscribe (like I do in this book).

## OTHER BOOKS

If you've published, or will soon publish, other titles, you MUST list those inside your book. Unless you have dozens of them, use thumbnails. This list will be most effective if you have a series or if your other books are in the same genre. But even if they're not, you should still mention them. Your reader might be a fan of multiple genres!

## PICTURE AND BIO

See the Product section.

## TARGET AUDIENCE

Before we go into the various promotional techniques (and I know you can't wait!), we have to identify our target audience and where our readers 'hang'. I use a very sneaky tool to do it.

First of all, I identify competing titles and authors and then I go to Facebook Audience Insights to find out who my audience is.

## ONLINE

### WEBSITE

Your online home, your hub, your kingdom is your website. A professional author's website has the author's name in its domain. If you're rolling your eyes because your website's domain is your book's title, please consider this: you're an author, right? So you will write another book and another, and another, and another. Are you going to create a new website each time? No. I learned this the hard way... but I'm here to help you save some time: buy your NameSurname.com domain or, if it's taken, buy it from the owner for $10,000. Just kidding. If your name-surname domain is taken, get the AuthorNameSurname.com domain or a variation.

Now that you have your domain, build a professional website.

1)   The first thing you need is a sign-up form. You want those readers on your list and you have to give them something exciting in exchange.
2)   About your books page: obvious.

3) About you: with a funny, memorable bio and a professional author picture.
4) Testimonials: copy paste all the editorial reviews you've received or even your best Amazon reviews.
5) Links to social media, but not too many (this is a fine art).

Feel free to check out my website for readers at http://alinkarutkowska.com if you're looking for inspiration. I used OptimizePress (http://alinkarutkowska.com/optimizepress) to create it.

I'm not the only one with these views on effective author website. Jane Friedman (notice the domain name!) agrees: http://janefriedman.com/2012/02/27/effective-author-website/

## EMAIL MARKETING

This is where the fun begins! I am providing you here with a mile-long laundry list of what works, but if I was forced to pick only one marketing tool, this would be it.

Social media is great, and we will go through it in a bit, but you don't own any of those networks. Cracking Amazon's algorithm sounds enticing but they can change it whenever they want. Guest blogging is cool but your host can take that post down at their whim. Bottom line is you don't own social media, other blogs, or retail sites but you do own your email list.

Additionally, when you send out an email each of your respondents will see it (unless it ends up in their spam but this is unlikely). On the contrary, if you update your Facebook page, less than five percent of your followers will ever see it. But that's obvious. Facebook's objective is to have people spend more time on their site and what people want to see is what their friends are up to, not what you want to promote, so Facebook can and is limiting the reach of those posts drastically.

But your mailing list is truly yours. You decide when and what to send and there are so many ways you can play with this tool. This is where your creative brain can shine!

Below are ten ways I used to increase my list from zero (we all start from scratch) to thousands of subscribers:

1. **Permafree:** I published a permanently free book and in it I have a call to action: if readers click through to my website and subscribe, they will get another free book (yes, you need two free books, or one free book and something else your readers dig - for free). About 5-10 percent of the people

who download your book will subscribe. This is a completely free strategy. It's also a good idea to write a trilogy and make the first book permafree ;)

2. **Wattpad**: As a children's author I only recently discovered Wattpad and it's fantastic. If you're going to publish a book for free, why not post chapters on Wattpad and have your biggest fans subscribe to your list? I recently finished my first novel (fantasy, under a pen name) and I follow people who follow other fantasy authors. Some follow me back, read my story and the most engaged ones subscribe to my list because I tell them I will give them a free copy of the book once it's published. This is free strategy (but time-consuming).

3. **StoryCartel:** You can go to their website and offer your book for free on their site. Readers can download and leave you a review. That's actually the purpose of this site but you do get their email addresses so you build your list! They also have a paid option - they can send info about your book to their mailing list.

4. **NoiseTrade:** List your book on their site and have hundreds of readers download your book. You will get their email address. Of course some people are freebie seekers and will unsubscribe as soon as you send

them their first newsletter but a good chunk (the majority) will stay.

5. **Content Marketing:** Like blogging? Consistently write helpful content and get your readers to subscribe to your newsletter by asking them at the end of your article or with a pop-up.

6. **Goodreads:** Contact people who reviewed books similar to yours. Have them go through a sign up form before you give them your free book (this works well with launches).

7. **Amazon:** Contact Amazon reviewers who reviewed books similar to yours. Use the same strategy you use for Goodreads. Remember to only contact reviewers who favorably reviewed other books.

8. **Facebook Ads:** Promote your freebies and your content with Facebook ads. Respond to all comments people write on your ad. Direct people to your sign up form and monitor your performance with Website Conversions.

9. **Twitter Ads:** They are not as sophisticated as Facebook ads but some authors manage to build their lists successfully through them at a lower cost than on Facebook.

10. **Giveaways:** See below.

Whatever you do, never add people manually to your list. They will most likely unsubscribe and complain. Also every subscriber has a cost, so you really don't want people not interested in your content on your list.

### GIVEAWAYS

Giveaways are a fantastic way to increase your subscriber list, if you know how to run them.

**Here's how to do it:**

**1) Figure out a prize** that will be relevant to your readers. I don't recommend giving away cash, iPads or Kindles because you will get plenty of subscribers who don't care about your books and you will end up having to pay for them with your email provider and you won't get any value from them.

The prize I recommend is a bunch of your books or a combination of yours and those of similar authors. A prize of over $100 is best, so around 10 great books from your genre (including your book) would do well.

**2) Choose the right platform.** Here are some popular choices:

1 **Rafflecopter** - it's free and you can run it on any website. What I don't love about it is that it shows the number of entries. If the number is low, the reader will think "nobody's entering this giveaway so why should I?" and when it gets high she could think "my chance of winning is really low now so why bother?" but since it's free it gives you an idea of what a giveaway is and you can select a better solution in the future.

2 **KingSumo** - this platform runs only on a WordPress site and it was designed to grow subscriber lists. It has an incredible conversion rate (almost everybody who lands on the giveaway page enters the giveaway) and it promotes sharing - if you share the giveaway, you get more entries - and so the word spreads. This is what I am using at the moment. There's a one-off fee.

3 **UpViral** - I hear it's the latest and greatest in giveaway software, you can use it on any website and integrate it with your Facebook page. You can use it not only for giveaways but also for viral contests and viral product launches. The great thing about it is that it integrates with every email service provider so you don't have to copy and paste the

subscribers to your lists manually.
There's a monthly fee.

**3) Promote your giveaway.** I know, crazy,
right? Not only are you giving stuff for free but
you also have to pay to promote this!
Unfortunately, yes. Here's how:

1   There's a bunch of websites you can
    use to promote your giveaway, the most
    popular being givewawaypromote.
    There's a list of sites you can submit
    your giveaway to at http://
    makobiscribe.com/for-the-blogger/
    places-to-submit-your-giveaways/. And if
    you want somebody to do it for you, you
    can get the dirty work outsourced at
    https://www.onlinejobs.ph.

2   Contact influencers and get them to
    tweet or post about your giveaway on
    Facebook. Think who would be a great
    person to talk about your giveaway and
    approach them. Offer them one or all of
    your giveaway prizes in exchange. If
    you have some kind of following, cross-
    promotion might work. On rare
    occasions people do this for a fee.

3   You can also promote your giveaway
    with Facebook ads but if your giveaway
    is running for a short time, you might not

have enough time to test your ads to get the lowest cost per click.

**4) Engage your subscribers.** This is crucial. As soon as somebody enters your giveaway start them on a series of autoresponders so that they get to know you. Start by thanking them for entering the giveaway in the first email and follow up by introducing yourself and your books. Remember always to respond to any questions your readers might have. If they took the time to write an email to you, treat them like celebrities — they are the reason you will thrive as an author.

## EMAIL SIGNATURE

It's show time! As an author actively marketing your books you will send out massive amounts of email, so make the most of your email signature! While signing off as 'Galactic President Superstar McAwesomeville' might be a slight exaggeration, do use any honors you've received.

But that's not all. Once you've got that email list live and kicking, your email signature is the perfect place to entice your readers to sign up for it!

You know the theory, now go put into practice. You can take my signature and modify it so that it works best for you.

**Alinka Rutkowska**
Multi-Award-Winning, #1 International Best-Selling Children's Author

*PARENTS* - Get your FREE children's book here.
*AUTHORS* - Get your FREE video training! Go here.

## AMAZON

Before you start promoting your book with full force and speed make sure that your number one retailer author page is working for you and not against you.

Go to author central at https://authorcentral.amazon.com, go to the Author Page tab and update your biography. Make it short and memorable and you MUST add a link to your website and give your readers a reason to click through! I say "COME OVER, I sometimes give books away for FREE!"

Add a professional author photo, your blog feed and Twitter feed. Then go to the Books tab and add all your books.

We'll talk about Amazon reviews in the Reviews section.

## PICK YOUR SOCIAL MEDIA

According to *Digital Marketing Ramblings* at http://expandedramblings.com/index.php/resource-how-many-people-use-the-top-social-media/ there are over 700 top social media, apps and digital services you could be using to promote your book. Which ones will you use? How will you choose?

Of course we need to go after the most popular ones that gather *readers.* Even this shortlist, however, might be too overwhelming. Whenever I find myself wondering which marketing task I should perform next I think to myself, "What would Vilfredo do?"

Vildredo Pareto was an Italian economist who observed in 1906 that 80 percent of the land in Italy was owned by 20 percent of the population. He also noticed that 20 percent of the pea pods in his garden contained 80 percent of the peas. Thus, the Pareto principle also known as the 80-20 rule. So whenever I find myself overwhelmed I make sure that I do the 20 percent of the tasks on my list that will yield 80 percent of results.

In other words, I picked my social media focusing on Facebook, Twitter and Goodreads;

the 20 percent that brings me 80 percent of my results.

## FACEBOOK

As we mentioned in the Email Marketing section, Facebook has its reasons to limit the reach of your fan page posts to around five percent, and I've observed that one percent is a more accurate number. The main reason is that Facebook wants to stay cool to its users. But don't worry, not all is lost. There is a way to get your message in front of your target audience. It's called Facebook Ads.

Facebook is an absolutely amazing database. Each time I create an ad and select my target audience I marvel at all the information gathered about the users (which folks put up voluntarily). This Facebook feature allows me to identify my audience precisely and get to know them down to their household income (I'm not kidding you!).

If, however, you wish to do without ads (I don't recommend this), you might be interested in joining one of the many Facebook groups for authors to promote your book:

Indie Author Book Promotion Page (26K members)

https://www.facebook.com/groups/571135069563269/

Amazon Kindle Goodreads (23K members)
https://www.facebook.com/groups/kindle.goodreads/?fref=nf

Authors and Book Lovers Discussion Group (22K members)
https://www.facebook.com/groups/authorspostyourbooks/875925592496142/?notif_t=group_activity

Free Books (19K members)
https://www.facebook.com/groups/2705583363796992/661142860654569/?notif_t=group_activity

Book Reviews & Promotion (18K members)
https://www.facebook.com/groups/148313988694907/?ref=br_tf

E-BOOK (18K members)
https://www.facebook.com/groups/Paoloebook/

Amazon book and ebook readers (18K members)
https://www.facebook.com/groups/419504758165134/?ref=browser

AMAZON BOOKS, LIKES AND RANKINGS (18K members)

https://www.facebook.com/groups/4430144452450161/

EbooksNBooksPromosGroup (17K members)
https://www.facebook.com/groups/eBooksBooksPromo/712959785475781/?notif_t=group_activity

Promote Your Book! (16K members)
https://www.facebook.com/groups/205686289555465/

FREE books R Us (15K members)
https://www.facebook.com/groups/freebkrus/877493308972307/?notif_t=group_activity

Celebrating Authors (14K members)
https://www.facebook.com/groups/157960580960255/

Kindle ... (14K members)
https://www.facebook.com/groups/acrebooks/

Amazon Kindle/ebook Readers UK/Europe/Asia/Africa/Elsewhere (11K members)
https://www.facebook.com/groups/129536203777715/944828622248465/?notif_t=group_activity

The New Writers (11K members)
https://www.facebook.com/groups/thenewwriters/

-->> PROMOTE Kdbook! FREE! (10K members)
https://www.facebook.com/groups/promotekdbook/1607590606173561/?notif_t=group_activity

BooksGoSocial Readers' Group (10K members)
https://www.facebook.com/groups/booksgosocialreaders/

Writers Like Writers (8K members)
https://www.facebook.com/groups/WritersLikeWriters/

Kindle Favorites - Discuss your favorite books on Amazon Kindle (7K members)
https://www.facebook.com/groups/kindle.favorites/?ref=browser

Indie Book Hangout (5K members)
https://www.facebook.com/groups/IndieBookHangout/

Amazon Kindle Books Authors & Readers Unite (4K members)
https://www.facebook.com/groups/KindleWorldAuthors/

amazon.it (2K members)

https://www.facebook.com/groups/
479120328793821/968841779821671/?
notif_t=group_activity

Clean Indie Reads (2K members)
https://www.facebook.com/groups/
cleanindiereads/

**TWITTER**

I've had a love/hate type of relationship with Twitter but since some of my posts had a huge boost from my Twitter activity and some libraries contacted me via this network wanting to stock my books, it's more of a love relationship now.

The main thing about Twitter is to use relevant hashtags in your posts. Once you've learned to do that people will start to follow you. Also provide funny or meaningful content, limiting your "buy my book" posts to a minimum.

Now here are some of those magical hashtags:

Reading Hashtags
#Books #BookWorm #GreatReads #IndieThursday #MustRead #Novel #Paperbacks #Storytelling #WhatToRead

ePublishing Hashtags

#Amazon #eBook #BookBuzzr #eReaders #ePubChat #iPad #kidlitchat #Kindle #KindleBargain #Kobo #KPD #Nook #Pubit #SmashWords #Sony #Webfic #YALitChat #Zinechat

Marketing Hashtags
#99c #AuthorRT #BookGiveaway #BookMarketing #FollowFriday #FreebieFriday #FreeReads

## GOODREADS

Facebook and Twitter might be huge but Goodreads is where the real bookworms 'hang'. That's where you can get readers for your email list, reviewers for your current and upcoming books, lifetime fans and repeat buyers.

The thing about Goodreads is that it's not very user friendly. It's hard to navigate and many authors just don't bother. Huge mistake! Just as email marketing is my number one marketing tool, Goodreads is my number one social network!

## OTHER SOCIAL MEDIA PLATFORMS:

I know that the social media world doesn't end with Facebook, Twitter and Goodreads but it's my 20 percent (see the Pareto Principle in the

Pick Your Social Media section). I'm present on other networks indirectly: I 'feed' my profiles with my blog feed. So all I need to do is write one blog post and automatically that will show up on ALL my social media sites. There are plug-ins for this.

One other platform that is worth mentioning is LinkedIn. I don't use it to connect with readers (although some do want to connect there as well). LinkedIn is what I use to connect with other industry professionals. That's how I find retail departments of companies I want to place my books in.

I think that every professional author should have a LinkedIn profile for these purposes.

## BLOG (AND FEED)

As mentioned several times above I like to post news updates on my blog simply because I own my blog and then I 'feed' my social media networks with these updates. My website is owned by me, whereas third party networks are not. Plus, I only need to create one post to have it appear on Facebook, Twitter, Google+, Amazon, Goodreads, LinkedIn and more.

The thing about blogging is that you need to find your rhythm and your voice. Are you going to do a long article once a week? Or are you going to do a short news update daily? It's all up to you. You can experiment as much as you like, just make sure you find your style and stick to it because once you start gaining readers they will expect you to stay consistent!

## GUEST BLOGGING

A great way to expand your reach and gain a new audience is to guest blog. Find an influential blogger with a big following, go through their stuff, like and comment on their posts and develop a relationship. After a while contact them telling them how you would love to provide them with a unique and meaningful article about a subject that is within their scope. Tell them how you will promote the s**t out of it and how they will be ever grateful to you (maybe skip that last part).

Make sure to add a link to your sign-up form within your article and give people a reason to subscribe.

This is a time consuming task, and it may or may not be within your 20 percent that brings you the most results. You need to set some time to research the right bloggers, read their websites, comment and approach them. You need to wait for their reply and then provide them with extraordinary material. Depending on the influence of your blogger, your post may bring you a substantial number of quality subscribers or the whole thing may become a total waste of time.

## BLOG TOURS

I've done several when I was still inexperienced and I thought they actually worked. I paid hundreds of green American money to these blog tour companies who prepared a month-long schedule for me which brought me maybe one additional purchase.

I was the one promoting the bloggers' sites. This didn't make sense. Not all was wasted though. This experience allowed me to say that I was featured here and there, so I used it as a springboard to bigger opportunities.

What does work and works exceptionally is a blog tour that you organize yourself. But you need to develop relationships with other influential authors and bloggers. If you can schedule a blog tour with influencers that you handpick, you can get yourself an amazing outcome. But this is extremely time-consuming and you might need to hire a virtual assistant to help you.

## KDP SELECT

When you subscribe to KDP Select (see the Price section) you get access to a few promotional tools you can use.

Free Book Promotions and Kindle Countdown Deals:

1) Free Book Promotions:

According to KDP at https://kdp.amazon.com/help?topicId=A34IQ0W14ZKXM9 *you can offer any book enrolled in KDP Select free to readers for up to five days at your discretion during each 90-day enrollment period in KDP Select.*

2) Kindle Countdown Deals:

According to the website at https://kdp.amazon.com/help?topicId=A3288N75MH14B8 *Kindle Countdown Deals is a new KDP Select benefit that lets authors provide readers with limited-time discount promotions on their books available on amazon.com and amazon.co.uk. It's a great opportunity to earn more royalties and increase discoverability of your book. Customers will see the regular price and the promotional price on the book's detail page, as well as a countdown clock showing how much time is left at the promotional price. You'll also continue to earn your selected royalty rate on each sale during the promotion.*

Authors' experience with these tools vary. Setting up a deal is not enough. You need to promote it big time. While there are many sites that you can promote your free or discounted book on (http://www.trainingauthors.com/47-places-to-submit-your-free-kdp-promotion-for-your-kindle-ebook/), BookBub is the real deal.

## BOOKBUB

"What is BookBub?" you ask. It's *the* place to be if you're doing a free or discounted promotion (see KDP Select above).

It's great if you schedule a promotion — but who's going to know about it? BookBub has a mailing list (I know, here we go again!) of MILLIONS of avid readers who love free and discounted books. The offer arrives straight to their inboxes and with a click of a button they can download or buy your masterpiece.

Here's what BookBub says about itself at https://www.bookbub.com/home/about.php:
*BookBub is a free service that helps millions of readers discover great deals on acclaimed ebooks while providing publishers and authors with a way to drive sales and find new fans. Members receive a personalized daily email alerting them to the best free and deeply discounted titles matching their interests as selected by our editorial team. BookBub works*

*with all major ebook retailers and devices, and is the industry's leading ebook price promotion service.*

Please note that when they say that they are a "free service" they mean that they are free for the readers receiving their updates. Here's the price list for us authors: https://www.bookbub.com/partners/pricing. As you see, depending on your genre and whether you go for the free or discounted promotion you will pay between $55 and $1,725.

How does it work? You submit your book for BookBub's consideration and then its *editorial team reviews your book and decides whether they'd like to select it for a feature* (see more at https://www.bookbub.com/partners/how-it-works).

While BookBub does list its requirements (https://www.bookbub.com/partners/requirements)
and tips
(https://www.bookbub.com/partners/submission-tips) for getting selected, so many authors have been rejected that the selection process is a bit of a mystery.

I've enrolled my books a couple of times in the past only to get a rejection letter but recently I received the following message from them: "Hi

Alinka, Good news! Our editorial team selected your title for a BookBub feature."

So what has changed? Several things:

1   Instead of being available only on KDP Select, my book is also on iTunes and Kobo.
2   It's got a professional cover, which is clearly visible in thumbnail size.
3   I was super flexible with dates.
4   I had several editorial reviews.
5   I launched it with over 100 reviews in 3 days and many of those reviewers featured the book on their blogs and social media.

**The results:**

I received several emails from authors asking about my financial results of the BookBub feature and here are my answers:

- *What was your return on investment (ROI)?* I invested $160 in this ad (children's category - $3.99 book discounted to $0.99). I sold 300 copies on Amazon on the day and the day after the promotion. If you're out of KDP Select, that's a revenue of 300x$0.35=$105. If you're in KDP Select, that's a revenue of 300x$0.70=$210. I also made some sales in other marketplaces: 10-20 bucks in total.

- **How long did you have residual sales at full price?** I treated this book as an experiment from day one and did no promotion for it whatsoever - only the BookBub ad. Before the ad, I was selling 0 copies a day, after the ad I averaged five copies on Amazon at a $3.99 price point (with no promotion).

- **What is the value of hitting the bestseller list, even if it's only for a short time like one day (can authors really boast that their books are bestsellers when that status is so fleeting and hinged on a half price sale?)?** I have hit #1 bestseller on Amazon before but never on three Amazon sites at the same time. Thanks to this promotion I can call myself a #1 International Best-Selling Author. Will I use this title? It depends where. I did put it on my new business cards because success leads to more success. I also put it on my catalogs, which I will be distributing at the Bologna Children's Book Fair at the end of the month. I also included it in my email signature. I know this is not the same as hitting the *New York Times* Best Sellers list but it's still an accomplishment and I believe it's one that you can be proud of, one that gives you self-confidence and one that you can use to attract more sales.

- **What other results did you have on top of the financial ones?** I got 20 new subscribers to my mailing list, a couple of reviews and the option to call myself a #1 International Best-Selling Author. (Even though I have sold around 80,000 books I couldn't call myself this and now I can!)

- **Can you share any best practices?** Of course! Make sure that inside the book you are promoting you have hyperlinks to your other books and to your sign-up form (especially if you're doing a free promotion).

- **Would you do it again with BookBub?** Yes, I will for the books I believe in most.

To sum up, BookBub promotion significantly boosts your sales rankings, gets you new readers and you will make your money back plus make some more if you go for the paid option.

## CONTACT LOCAL NEWSPAPERS, TV CHANNELS, RADIO

TV, radio and newspapers are no longer just for the super-famous. All media is constantly looking for news and local media is looking for local news. What you need to do is start early, find a hook that you can link to and contact your local radio, TV and newspapers.

You can also sign up for HARO at http://www.helpareporter.com. How does it work? Sources (you're a source) *will receive three emails a day, Monday through Friday at 5:35 a.m., 12:35 p.m. and 5:35 p.m. EST, with queries from reporters and media outlets worldwide. Scan the emails, and if you're knowledgeable about any of the topics, answer the reporter directly through the anonymous @helpareporter.net email address provided at the beginning of the query.*

I've received some elegant exposure thanks to this service but bear in mind that scanning through the emails and responding is time-consuming. It can, however, be very rewarding.

## PRESS RELEASE

Don't want to ask others for a feature? You can do it yourself! Get yourself a professionally crafted press release. Do it yourself and have it edited or get it done by a professional and then let the world know about it!

I've used and recommend iReach by PR Newswire at https://ireach.prnewswire.com/Home.aspx. It has accessible price options ranging from $129 to $399 (see https://ireach.prnewswire.com/orders/price-options.aspx).

You can tell the world about your new release, your awards or anything else you can come up with. You could even partner with other authors to split the cost and do a group press release.

I've seen a significant spike in my book sales after I've issued my own press releases, but your results will vary depending on who picks up your release, when you send it and many other factors.

Again, make sure you direct your readers to your website where they will find a sign-up form ;)

### VIDEO TRAILERS

I don't want to say that video trailers are dead but I haven't noticed any increased sales from mine.

What does work are videos that go viral but you need to know how to create those. Or... you can go to http://www.fiverr.com and hire someone who will create a funny video for you for not much more than $5! I've used Fiverr countless times for different jobs and some sellers really know their craft.

## GETTING PROFESSIONAL REVIEWS

It's great to have some professional reviews that you can include in your book description (within the book itself or as metadata — see the Product section). Where do you get them?

*Readers' Favorite* - FREE (also offers paid services) at https://readersfavorite.com/book-reviews.htm

*BookLife* by *Publishers Weekly* - FREE at http://booklife.com/about-us/reviews-faqs.html

*Kirkus Review* (https://www.kirkusreviews.com/author-services/indie/) - $425 to $575. Is it worth it? Joanna Penn wrote, "I once paid for a Kirkus Review for my first nonfiction book — but it was an expensive mistake. I wouldn't do that again!" See more here: https://selfpublishingpodcast.com/19/

*Clarion Review* - $499 at https://publishers.forewordreviews.com/reviews/
*Blue Ink Review* - $395 to $495 at http://www.blueinkreview.com

Here's a list of "Prolific Indie Reviewers": http://www.theindieview.com/indie-reviewers/

Once you've received a review you're proud of, insert it into your book description directly in your Author Central (or CreateSpace) and KDP dashboard and anywhere else you are distributing your book.

## GETTING PERSONAL REVIEWS

Reviews can make or break your book's success, and it's often not even the quality that counts but the quantity. The more you have, the more buzz your book will get and the more noteworthy it will appear in the eyes of your potential readers.

When I just started out, I noticed that I had to sell 2,000 books to get 20 unsolicited reviews, so it took a couple of months, and I was probably lucky to get so many.

Fewer than one percent of readers leave a review out of their own initiative. And since they are so important I've now developed a system for soliciting reviews from avid readers. I've perfected it to the point in which I now get 50+ reviews on launch day with minimum effort.

Before I get to my 'review recipe' I'd first like to direct all of you to the Amazon's top reviewer list at http://www.amazon.com/review/top-reviewers. Check who reviews books in your genre and contact them. Few authors know that the top reviewers compete with one another as to the number of reviews they write and the likes they receive for them. They are hungry to review your book! You will have to send them a free copy and some will want a paperback but it's just part of the deal. Use your best manners when approaching them.

Remember to put a request for review inside your book (see the Your Product's Add-ons section).

## REVIEW SWAPS

Authors often swap reviews. I've done it a couple of times but there is always one problem: what if they give you 5 stars and you only want to give them 3? It could also be the other way around. These are a little bit tricky but if you want to try it out, join any Facebook group for authors and try connecting with people one by one. I think it works best with authors writing in the same genre!

## BLOG TOURS

These are very popular. You pay an administration fee to a company, which organizes a blog tour for you and your book and as a result you will get some reviews. I've done two with two different companies and my results varied. One of them delivered all the posts and reviews (but I paid $400!) whereas the other one (which seemed better organized and had a better website) did not. You have to organize these in advance, prepare guest posts and interviews, so it's a lot of work but you will get some reviews (depending on how many blog stops you pay for!).

## CONNECTING WITH BLOGGERS ONE BY ONE

If you want to bypass the administration fees, you can try contacting bloggers by yourself. Google a competitor's book "+review" or "+blog tour" and you will then get a list of bloggers who featured it. You can then try contacting them one by one. Many of them will ignore you but some will reply and post reviews. It's a numbers game. The more people you contact, the more reviews you'll get.

Now, an even better way than contacting Amazon's top reviewers is contacting real avid readers, loving to read and reviewing books for pleasure as opposed to getting Amazon brownie points.

We've already talked about *the* social networks for READERS. It's Goodreads. Goodreads is the world's largest site for readers and book recommendations. It has 30 million members, 900 million books added and 34 million reviews. As you can see from these numbers, it has more reviews than members, meaning that on average a Goodreads user writes multiple reviews!

## 100 REVIEW BOOK LAUNCH

Thanks to all I learnt about reviews, I recently launched a book with 100 Amazon reviews in three days.

You can follow the steps below and get your reviews spread in time, or you can plan a big launch and get them all in a couple of days. That's up to you.

First some statistics and psychology: I got 112 reviews from a team of 260 launch team members, who signed up and committed to reviewing my book on launch day. That's over 40 percent, which is actually very high. Usually around one third of the people who commit to review a book, do so. Why? I don't know, maybe they lose interest or have other commitments but it's important to be aware of these numbers. When you have a specific number of reviews in mind, you have to get triple that number of people to agree to review your book.

In order to have a certain number of people to agree to review your book, you need to contact several times more people. Many will ignore your request so I think you need to ask roughly four times more people than you want on your launch team. Does this mean I contacted 1,000 people before getting 100 reviews? Probably.

So where do you get 1,000 potential reviewers interested in reading and reviewing your book?

Below is an estimate of where the 1,000 came from:

**50 percent** came from my activity on **Goodreads**. I have a special system which I use to find passionate reviewers (I describe it in detail at authorremake.com but it requires time (15 min a day once you've got everything set up). I've been doing this for several months before I got these people on my mailing list.

**10 percent** are **Amazon Top Reviewers**. I went to http://www.amazon.com/review/top-reviewers and I looked for people reviewing books in my genre. I also contacted reviewers who reviewed books similar to mine.

**10 percent** I got using the **Author Marketing Club** (http://alinkarutkowska.com/amc) **Reviewer Grabber** (it's a premium feature). This tool scans Amazon for reviewer emails and websites. You just insert the books you want the tool to scan and it does the work. I got over 100 people this way.

**10 percent** are **bloggers** who have featured me before or whom I approached specifically for this launch.

**5 percent** come from a mini-**blog tour**. Even though I'm not a huge fan of these, I got a very good offer from one of the bloggers I contacted and they delivered everything they promised.

**5 percent** came from **LibraryThing**. I ran a Member Giveaway giving away 100 e-copies. 50 people requested it and when I sent out the book I mentioned that I have this launch going on. 10 people signed up.

**5 percent** came from a free **KDP promo** I ran for another book. I have a call to action inside, which gets people on my mailing list and some of the thousands of people who downloaded the book when it was free (I promoted that fact) subscribed.

**5 percent** are **friends and fellow authors** (these are not review swaps) - people who support me and want to see me succeed.

**COST:**
$105 annually to use Author Marketing Club Reviewer Grabber (http://alinkarutkowska.com/amc)

$75 mini blog-tour (10 reviews and an interview)
$25 to advertise the KDP promo

**MORE COST, PRIZES:**
To get my launch team all excited about this launch, I put them in a draw, in which they can win some cool stuff:
$50 Amazon Gift Card
$20 for four $5 Amazon Gift Cards
$35 for 5 paperbacks + postage
I have some more e-gifts, which don't cost me anything (okay, they are in my fixed costs).

GRAND TOTAL: $310

**Important note:** I only sent out pdf copies, so that didn't cost me anything and I always contact people personally, using their first name and sometimes trying to connect with them in a way (e.g. "You're from New Zealand!? I love NZ! I met my husband on a cruise from Auckland to Sydney!")

Now in terms of time...it's time consuming but the satisfaction of launching a book with 100+ reviews... that's priceless!

And you know what the best part is? I have all these people's email addresses, so next time I launch a book, it will only take a couple of emails ;)

## WHAT IF YOU GET A NEGATIVE REVIEW?

Have you already received your first 1-star-review? If not, my guess is that your book hasn't received much exposure yet, because if it has, someone is bound to express their honestly cruel opinion.

I don't want to get too philosophical about this but I wouldn't sweat it - at all.

### Why is a bad a review a good thing?

- It only gives credibility to the positive reviews you've received. Otherwise people might think that it's just friends reviewing your work.
- Many books which have an equal number of positive and negative reviews are very controversial and as such they sell very well.
- It gives you feedback - there's probably some truth in it and you can use it to improve your work.

### How to diminish the impact of a bad review?

Even though we can grow tough skin and learn not to sweat it, we still want to diminish the impact of these reviews as much as possible.

How can we do it?

- First of all, never try to change the reviewer's mind. I once persuaded a reviewer to increase their rating from 1 star to 3 stars but if you've received a 2-star review or higher and try to negotiate it, you're probably going to annoy the reviewer and they are very likely to lower their rating.

- If you run a structured book launch which gives you over 100 reviews, like I did for my recent release, you will be able to identify that reviewer and delete them from your list. Just think of an inexpensive reward you want to give them, send an email to your list with the winners and the negative reviewers will identify themselves. Give them the prize and delete them from your lists so they don't contaminate your future launches.

- As soon as your first 5-star reviews arrive, ask your trusted colleagues and/or friends to "yes" those reviews on Amazon. This way these will be the first reviews that people see and they will be likely to "yes" them as well. Automatically the negative ones will be buried under the avalanche of positive reviews you receive.

Again, don't worry - look up your favorite book on Amazon - I'm sure it's got a couple of 1-star-reviews too!

## OFFLINE

### BUSINESS CARDS

You shouldn't ever leave your house without your business card, not even when you're throwing out the trash.

Create two-sided cards.

On one side you will have a 'headline' describing the genre or uniqueness of your books with your website and some memorable artwork.

On the other side you will have your professionally done author picture with your name, job description (this is where you can say you are an "award-winning" or "best-selling" author, if you are!), and add your website and contact information.

Make it simple and easy to read AND, of course, add a link to your subscription form, and tell your readers what goodies you have waiting for them after they've subscribed.

I use http://www.vistaprint.com to create my business cards.

## BROCHURES

Very quickly you will realize that you need brochures. These will have your author picture on them, your bio, website and a list of your books with all the necessary details.

You will need these when you start negotiating to get your books into physical stores and when you go to book fairs.

## WORD OF MOUTH

If you're an introvert, that's fine, but as soon as someone asks you about your book, you have to know what to say. Prepare your 'elevator pitch' in case an important decision-maker wants to know more about your titles. Make sure you can present yourself in excellent light in less than a minute.

It also helps if you ALWAYS carry your book with you (for display purposes, not necessarily to sell).
Give out your business cards to everybody who asks about your book and tell them that you have some great goodies waiting for them if they subscribe to your mailing list (you can spare the top executives from this last line but nobody else).

## BOOK FAIRS

Book fairs are a great way to gain exposure. Getting a booth at a fair is, however, very expensive, and it's very unlikely that you'll sell enough books to cover the expense (especially at the big world-wide known events).

What I like to do is get my book displayed by a third party and go to the fair to mingle and make connections, not to sell. I hand out my business cards and brochures to readers and I develop strategic connections with people from the industry.

Each book fair is different but you will usually be able either to share a stand with other authors (and split the cost) or get your books to be featured by someone else. The latter might be a service you can purchase or something completely complimentary like representation at the International Miami Book Fair by Readers' Favorite for all the winners of the contest.

Do research the local book fairs well in advance and make sure you attend equipped with your cards and brochures and check that your books are featured.

What I like most about the big book fairs is that it's a great opportunity to sell foreign rights.

## FOREIGN RIGHTS

*You want your book to travel the world and find new audiences who love to discover a new story.*

I love the above sentence.
It comes from https://publishers.forewordreviews.com/trade-shows/, a service I use to get my books displayed at the big fairs.

Here's what I do:

**1. First of all you should have your books displayed at the fair.** If you are traditionally published, negotiate with your publisher. If you are independently published, you have two options:

- You can get a stand and sit there hoping that someone will come over and express interest in your books. You can throw a couple of thousand dollars at it and sit there yourself or you can find other authors (collective stand) and share the cost. The pro is that you can potentially sell your books there but that's not what those fairs are for, and you'd probably sell just a few copies anyway. The con is that you can't move from your stand and it will most probably be located off the main halls were the serious business happens. I don't recommend this approach (I've done it in the past and I learnt the hard way).

- You can get your books displayed by a third party like Foreword Reviews or The American Collective Stand. This is the approach I recommend.

**2. Go to the fair.** Go check out your book displayed at the fair and start talking to the people representing it. That's how I scored a foreign rights agent. Come equipped. You need catalogues, business cards and possibly a poster. At the Bologna Book Fair there's a huge wall where you can stick your poster. Then interested parties photograph this wall and someone might fall in love with your work this way!

**3. Go scout.** It's show time. Now that you have your poster on the wall, the people displaying your book equipped with your catalogues, the hard work starts. You want to get foreign publishers to buy your book rights. You have hundreds of publishers right there, so it can get a little overwhelming. Here's what you do:

- Approach a stand and check out their books. See if your titles would be a good fit for that publisher. I usually start right off the bat, asking if they are potentially interested in acquiring foreign rights.

Some will say that they only want to sell, not buy. No problem, move on.

- If they say yes, tell them that you checked out their books (on the shelves) and that you think your work might be a good fit for them. Ask them if you can show them your books.

- They will usually say yes. Now it's time to brag. Whip out your books and catalogues and start your pitch. I always mention three things:

1 **The awards the books received.** Publishers are very excited if your books are award winning. They loved the Readers' Favorite Book Awards I received.

2 **That my books are #1 Amazon best-sellers** in their categories and that I managed to get 100 reviews in 3 days for my latest releases. Publishers were VERY impressed by this.

3 **My sales in absolute numbers.** This is optional and it gets better over time. If you have substantial sales or if you have already sold rights to other countries, do tell!

- If you see that the publisher is interested, leave them your catalogue. If you see that they are VERY interested, leave them a copy of your book. Always ask for their contacts (acquisition editor) and then follow up after the fair. If you have a foreign rights agent, give the contacts to them and they will follow up.

The scouting is very tiring and requires a completely different set of skills than writing a book does. But you get better with every pitch.

**A few tips:**
- If possible, bring an assistant (or friend) who will scout for you as well - you will get much more done much faster.
- A series sell. Publishers like having a series and they might want to buy your whole catalogue (yes, it happens!).
- Don't get discouraged. If one publisher says your book is not for them, move on. The next one might be over the moon about your ideas.
- Ask for advice. If publishers don't like your books, ask them why and how you could improve. Ask them what they are looking for and you might be able to provide them exactly that the following year.
- Dress smart. First impressions count - be professional.

- Wear comfortable shoes - there's a lot of walking involved.
- Have fun! You're supposed to be enjoying this, you're getting your work out there, it's exciting!

**The trade shows in 2017 are as follows:**
American Library Association Midwinter Conference, January 20 - 24, 2017, Atlanta, GA;

Bologna Children's Book Fair, April 3 - 6, 2017, Bologna, Italy;

BookExpo America, May 31 - June 2, 2017, Chicago, IL;

American Library Association Conference & Exhibition, June 22 - 27, 2017, Orlando, FL;

Beijing International Book Fair, August 23 - 27, 2017, Beijing, China;

Frankfurt Book Fair, October 11 - 15, 2017, Frankfurt, Germany;

China Children's Book Fair, Dates TBD, Shanghai, China.

You might also simply be approached by a foreign publisher with a request to buy the rights to your books (that's how I got one of my books translated into Turkish!). Remember to read the contract or, better yet, get a lawyer to read through it. If you have a foreign rights agent, have them handle it. They will take a percentage but they know what they're doing.

You might also want to approach foreign publishing houses independently. Of course, you can do that, but I don't recommend it. It's way too time consuming, and you'll be much better off by sending your book over to relevant trade fairs where hungry foreign publishers gather to find new books for their collections.

As mentioned above, I had my book featured by Foreword Reviews at the Bologna Children's Book Fair in early 2014, which I attended. I networked a little and met my future foreign rights agent. I then featured a book from the series at the China Children's Book Fair the same year and a few months later I got an offer from a Chinese publisher wanting to buy rights, not to one book, but to all 15 books from the series! The joy of my expanding world domination was the biggest reward (the Chinese market is a big one and when they print your titles, it's on a big scale). The handsome advance was the icing on the cake!

## BOOK SIGNING

Opinions about book signings vary. Some authors think they work wonders and claim to sell books by the truckload, others don't get any results. It all depends on where and when your book signing is but most of all it depends on how approachable you are. If you just sit there and play with your phone, nobody will come over but if you stand and smile and welcome people to your stand, of course readers will start arriving.

It always helps to wear a funny costume or something that will make you stand out. It's a great icebreaker and will help you network with your readers and sell your books.

You can have a book signing pretty much anywhere and the hosts will happily have you if you can prove that you will drive traffic to their outlets.

Don't just limit yourself to the big bookstores. Think of independent stores, libraries, schools, coffee shops, bars, restaurants — anything that is somehow thematically linked to your book. I know authors who sell thousands of books this way (but they do a lot of events!).

Start local (local entrepreneurs will happily host a local author) and then expand your reach.

What I love most about book signings is that you get to know your target audience in person. You can talk to them, answer their questions, see what they're looking for and maybe you'll even get inspired to create a brand new title or even series based on their feedback!

## PUBLIC SPEAKING

Last but not least, public speaking works. If you can first show your crowd that you really know what you're talking about, you can then easily sell your books at the back of the room.

The thing with public speaking is that you have to get over yourself, so start small. Do a little speech somewhere local and then expand.

It might not be for everybody but it can become an important source of revenue (as you grow you will be able to charge handsome amounts just for the speaking itself!).

## WARNING - CON ARTISTS

The author marketing world is full of wonderful opportunities, some of which you have never even imagined possible. And here's the place where I need to warn you. If you get an out-of-the blue proposal for a TV appearance, book contract, anything — stay alert. If it turns out that you need to pay some production fee, alarm bells should go off in your head.

Basically, if you get any proposal that you haven't actively solicited, it could be a scam. So search the Internet with the title of the company + scam, get a lawyer to look at the contract you're supposed to sign and stay safe. These are rare instances, but they do occur.

# FINAL POINTS

## CROWDFUNDING

I know that producing and marketing your book is expensive, and you will need a significant budget even if you're doing it the low cost way. But I don't think that authors should be penalized just because they're not doing it the get-100-rejections-first-traditional-way.

There is a quite new and very underutilized tool that authors can use and get something akin to a massive advance! It's called crowdfunding. You need to be very cautious though. You can't just launch a campaign and leave it. Many of them fail, and the reason is lack of preparation. But if you do learn how it's done, you can amass a significant amount that will allow you to produce a high quality book and market it effectively. It will allow you to produce and market a whole series successfully!

## SERIES

Now that you've found some success with your first book, it's time to write another, and another, and another, possibly turning them into a series. The more books you have, the bigger your reach, the more you can play with promotions for your readers and the sooner you will be able to become a full-time author — one who can make a comfortable living out of their books alone!

## FURTHER READING

Out of all the books I've read on writing and book marketing these are the most memorable:

### On Marketing

*How to Make a Living with your Writing* by Joanna Penn ($2.99)

*Write. Publish. Repeat.* by Sean Platt and Johnny B. Truant ($5.99)

*Let's Get Visible* by David Gaughran ($4.99)

*Your First 1000 Copies* by Tim Grahl ($5.99)

*Reader Magnets* by Nick Stephenson (Free)

*Book Reviews that Sell* by Gary Webb ($0.99)

### On Writing

*On Writing* by Stephen King ($11.99)

*Bird by Bird* by Anne Lamott ($11.99)

### Inspirational

*You Are a Writer* by Jeff Goins ($0.99)

## **FURTHER LEARNING**

It's important to keep learning in the indie author world. Things change quickly and the best way to stay up to date is to read newly released books for authors and attend various online and offline events.

Last year I participated in the Author Marketing Live Summit, which was an initiative of the <u>Author Marketing Institute</u> and after listening to 19 excellent speakers I have some key learnings to share with you.

1   Each author-speaker was unique and found a different path to success.

2   There were some key points that many speakers stressed, one of the most important ones was the need to build an author platform, starting with an email list.

3   There was a lot of talk about optimizing books for Amazon and understanding that Amazon is not just a book store but a search engine. As such there are some aspects of our Amazon presence which we can control, such as keywords. Remember that you can change your keywords at any time. I

dedicate a full lesson to keywords at authorremake.com.

4    Out of all the online stores Amazon is the most indie-friendly, considering in their algorithm not only sales but also date published, number of reviews, key words and others. Amazon also allows authors to compete in narrower niches than the other stores.

5    There was some mention about effective ways of getting reviews but I'm proud to say that we've already covered all of them (or more) at authorremake.com so you are all set :)

6    Several authors talked about making one of your books permafree in order to drive traffic to your mailing list and this is something I will be doing with one of my titles.

7    We talked about speaking gigs being a very lucrative possibility for authors, particularly those publishing nonfiction.

8    Some things work better for certain authors, so it's important to test what is working for you to see where your sales are coming from and what to tweak.

9   I enjoyed one of the speakers mentioning that actually having a book on the world's greatest store is a huge deal that we often take for granted, because that's just what we do as authors, we write books. But it's true - for many people it *is* a huge deal and we should take pride in what we are doing :)

10   One of the most important things in all this is to love what we are doing and if we're not, to do something else. Because when we love what we're doing, then even choosing the right key words for our books can be an enjoyable task.

# BONUS

What better way to succeed than to replicate best-selling authors' strategies.

I interviewed six authors to find out how they achieved their success. Read on to find out what they have in common, how they differ and what you have in common with them.

## Interview with S.L. Morgan

S. L. Morgan is one of us and her books are wildly successful. Below she shares the keys to her success, her struggles, her writing habits, her marketing strategies, her view of self-publishing and much more. I feel honored that she is a regular reader of my newsletter and that I had the privilege to interview her.

**BIO:** S.L. Morgan is the multi-award-winning and best-selling author of the new novel series, *Ancient Guardians*. She loves to interact with readers and other authors. When she is not on adventures in other dimensions or galaxies with her characters, she is enjoying time with her family. She finds her escape through reading, writing, and getting out to the lake on her boat. You can contact her at: ancientguardians2012@gmail.com

You can also find her at www.slmorganauthor.com (purchase links to the books are on this site. The first book is FREE!)

**Why do you write?**

Writing is my escape. I love creating new worlds, new adventures, and being involved in the lives of my characters. Writing is very therapeutic for me, and I enjoy the freedom that creating a fictional novel brings.

**How long have you been writing?**

I started writing in October 2011. I have always been an elaborate storyteller, but it wasn't until one day, after reading and re-reading various novels and trying to find new ones to capture my interest, that I felt a calling to write a series of my own. There is a quote that I love, and I am unsure of the author, but it suits why I began writing perfectly: "If you can't find a book you want to read, write one." The *Ancient Guardians* novel series is the result of my desperately wanting to find something unique and different from everything out there, and with the inspiration of my love for fantasy novels and classic romance, I began writing and haven't looked back since.

**How long have you been in the self-publishing business?**

I self-published my first novel in the Ancient Guardians series in December 2011.

**Is writing/publishing your full-time job? If not, what is?**

In a way, yes. I am a stay-at-home mom (we all know that *is* a job *wink*) but, with all of my kids in school now, I utilize that free time to write.

**What is your daily work schedule?**

Up at 5 a.m. Coffee is first on the 'to-do' list. After that, school lunches. Once the kiddos are up and off to school, I open the laptop, and I'm either writing or editing in my book series. At 3 p.m., I say goodbye to my imaginary friends and begin helping with homework and start prepping dinner. Sounds exciting, right? Actually, it is. Writing, just like reading, gives me some place to go when I can't necessarily go anywhere.

**What is the best writing advice you've ever gotten (or read)?**

"You can't make everyone happy!" This truly is the best advice I could ever have received as a writer. I've learned that not everyone loves what I love. My first book is a perfect example of that. (Fortunately, it has a wonderful approval rating, but there are some who love to vocalize how awful it was). As a young, published author, I let reviews dictate what I should or shouldn't put in my books. This is where writer's block hit me. Then, I received the best advice ever..."You can't make everyone happy." I also started noticing this with my book reviews. This actually happens all of the time with my first, second, and third novel. One reviewer will come in and slam the book for the romance in it. They hated the hero, he was too sappy! Then, directly after that, more reviews started coming in expressing their love for the romance in the book and the hero becoming their new book boyfriend. So in order to keep this short, I learned very quickly that what one hates another will love. Don't let negative reviews get you down, just smile and think to yourself, "My book wasn't for them, but it definitely was for the 80 percent of reviewers that absolutely loved it." With this said, write from your heart, for you and your writing will be pure and absolutely believable. Stay true to your work and to yourself.

**What is the best marketing advice you've ever gotten (or read)?**

After I published my first book, I needed a way to get it off of the back of the book shelves. It was very consistent in sitting in the 200,000+ rankings. I utilized KDP Select in order to increase downloads and get my book out there, hoping to get my name out there. It worked, but I didn't like the fact that my book was locked in with Amazon in order to utilize this feature. I WANTED my book out there. (KDP may work for you, and there are a lot of sites that help authors get their books to best seller status after running a KDP promotion, but I will be honest, it didn't work for me). I sent my book out on blog tours, which helped get me honest and detailed reviews. The next thing I knew, readers were asking why they couldn't find my book on NOOK or iTunes. NOTE: This advice I used works best if you have multiple novels. To get to the point quickly, I will say one word, PERMAFREE. Obviously, I couldn't use this until my second book was published, and once it was, I worked like crazy to get my first book FREE. Helpful hint if you're trying to use this: Goodreads has a group that will help you get this done in under a week. You just have to be willing to help other authors in playing the fun game of 'tell us about a lower price'. There is a process in order to do this. Get out of your exclusive contract with Amazon KDP. Upload your ebook to Smashwords (make sure your ebook is professionally formatted in order to pass Smashwords premium books). Set your price FREE. Once Smashwords or BookBaby sends your books out to all of the major retailers, this is when you either ask all of your family and friends to tell Amazon about your book's lower price, or get in with the Goodreads group that will help you tell Amazon about your free book. YOUR BOOK IS FREE!!! Enjoy and watch your rankings skyrocket and start back feeding your other books. It's that easy, right? Well, sort of. I'll explain below in the next question on how to utilize PERMAFREE to the best advantage.

**What has been your best marketing decision so far?**

This follows the above question. First, I invested and took the BIG risk of putting my book in the wonderful Reader's Favorite contest. I nearly fell out of my chair when I learned I was a finalist. This is where I had the privilege of meeting Alinka and many other wonderful talented authors. We all wait on pins and needles for the final results, and I was speechless when I learned my first book took silver in its category. During this time, I had done free book promotions like crazy (Booksends, BooksButterfly... Alinka has a wonderful list of resources for sites that promote your free book). My rankings took off. Then I noticed something with my competition. They were ranked number 1 in subcategories that Amazon never allowed me to pick. (Here's another CRITICAL side note: When you see a book in a subcategory that you can't pick when you publish your book on Amazon, simply copy and paste the entire subcategory list and email Amazon letting you know you want your book in: Fiction > Romance > Fantasy > Urban >

Legendary > My Book is Better Than the Rest category. Obviously, I made the last category up, but I hope you get the point. Amazon will do this for you without question, and the next thing you know, your book is a best seller in a subcategory and getting it out there even further.Why did I bring up that award again? Well, the BEST marketing decision I made was not to give up on BookBub. Have you heard of this amazing site that only a handful of authors can get accepted into? If you haven't, you're hearing about it now. BookBub is extremely selective with who they pick to run a promo for. Where no one really knows their selection process, I learned quickly after I won that award and they picked my book up for a promotion that the award helped. I had petitioned them to promote my books only to be rejected at least five times before I won the award. (Twice now). This promotion BLEW my mind. Obviously, knowing that I had the BookBub promotion coming up, I started setting up other FREE promotions with other sites. The day the promotions were set to go, I reached #2 in ALL of FREE kindle downloads and was blown away to watch that my 2nd and 3rd books started climbing the rankings as well. This permafree marketing has helped to keep me on Amazon's best-selling list, my author platform has grown, and best of all, it's FREE marketing. Today I sit in amazement watching all three of my books competing with traditional publishing houses, and I am so grateful that I have the opportunity to utilize the PERMAFREE option.

**What has been your worst decision as a writer and how did you bounce back?**

The worst decision I made as a writer was when I rushed to publish my first book. I had no idea that even though I paid a professional editor to edit and perfect it, I needed to at least have a few of my avid reader fans and friends help to beta test and proof it. This was extremely embarrassing and there are 1-star reviews still attached to that book to help me never forget one of the greatest mistakes I could have made. It is crucial to you, your book, and potential readers that you take your time and ensure that you are delivering the best quality book possible. I go beyond the editing and reading quality now, and I use a professional ebook formatter, and I also ensure that my covers are professional and unique. This will help you stand out from the rest, and yes, everyone judges a book by its cover. As an Indie author, I know I have to prove a lot to readers, and ensuring that every part of my book is top notch is critical.

**Do you think of yourself as an author or as an entrepreneur?**

I am an author first. If I can't write an intriguing novel, there is no way I am going anywhere with marketing it and building a fan base. I have noticed lately that I wear quite a few hats in this business. I believe you have to be both but it is critical that both are a passion for you or you will burn out. Every day I am looking for new advice on how to market my books and learning how other authors are doing it. Alinka has been a huge inspiration for me and has offered priceless information. I owe a debt of gratitude to her and other authors that were willing to share their secrets to help me learn more about being an entrepreneur in this writing business.

**What have been the key factors to your success?**

Having a positive attitude and never giving up. I look at the 'wonderful world of readers' so differently now, and whether or not they love or hate my work, I am grateful they took the time to recognize it. I deeply believe that a positive attitude will take you farther than you can imagine.

**What do you think traditional publishers should learn from self-publishers?**

Price point! Self-publishers are on a trend right now and beating out traditional publishing housed because they can offer sales on their books, do permafree in order to increase traffic, and back-selling to other books they have published. I have noticed that readers are finding a happy place in the $2.99-3.99 price range. It's difficult for the traditional publishers to meet this price point, unless, of course, it is a very popular book.

**What should self-publishers learn from traditional publishers?**

To have flawless and perfectly polished novels for readers to enjoy, this is what really separates the indie authors from the publishing houses. I understand we don't have a team of editors editing our books, but it is our duty to ensure it looks like we do.

**What do you think the publishing landscape will look like in five years?**

In my opinion, I truly believe that the self-publishing world will take over. I kind of think we are seeing it now. I truly believe that the publishing houses are watching Indie authors and how their work is received in order to take a chance on a book. I honestly can say right now that I am happy with where I am at as a self-published author not splitting my royalties with a major publishing house. I am also hearing of traditionally published authors getting out of their contracts and becoming self-published authors in order to keep more of their royalties and have more control over their books. We shall see, but the trends are sure heading toward a self-published new reading world.

**Please share some words of encouragement to authors who are still struggling.**

Don't give up. Just keep writing and do what you love. There are so many other authors that are in your shoes. I have been there, and I just had to look away and continue writing. I'm glad I did. Also, there are many authors out there that blog about this struggle. They are so uplifting and encouraging and are willing to offer you advice on how they dealt with it and how they climbed that mountain. Stay strong and write on!

**Thank you!**

## Interview with Carol Bodensteiner

An overnight success - this is how many would define Carol Bodensteiner's independently published novel, which was picked up by a traditional publisher, re-launched on July 7 and is now on top of the charts.

## How exactly did that happen?

I'm honored to have been able to interview Carol and get her to talk about everything that led to this big event.

**BIO:** Carol Bodensteiner is a writer who finds inspiration in the places, people, culture and history of the Midwest. Born in Iowa and raised on her family's dairy farm, Carol grew up with a love of the land and an appreciation for family that form the foundation of her writing. A graduate of the University of Northern Iowa and Drake University, Carol built a successful career in public relations consulting before turning to creative writing. She is a regular participant in the University of Iowa Summer Writing Festival. Carol blogs about writing, her prairie, gardening, and whatever in life interests her at the moment. Her writing has been published in several anthologies. She published a memoir *Growing Up Country: Memories of an Iowa Farm Girl* in 2008. Her debut novel *Go Away Home* - indie published in

2014 - was acquired by Lake Union Publishing and re-launched in July 2015.

**Your self-published book *Go Away Home* has been picked up by Lake Union (An Amazon Imprint) and is now on top of the charts! This is a spectacular success but let's start from the beginning:**

**How long have you been writing?**

I've been writing all my life, but until about 10 years, ago, the emphasis was business writing. I spent my career in marketing and public relations (useful background for an author), promoting products for my clients. Gradually, I felt the pull to creative writing, and I've focused on creative nonfiction and fiction since 2005.

**How long have you been in the self-publishing business?**

I embarked on self-publishing in 2007 when I published my memoir *Growing Up Country: Memories of an Iowa Farm Girl.* I learned so much, enjoyed the process, and achieved sales success, so when it came time to publish my debut novel *Go Away Home*, I never hesitated to indie publish again.

**Is writing/publishing your full-time job? If not, what is?**

Since I left a full-time job – and a full-time paycheck – more than five years ago, I don't think about full-time in the way I once did. My life is full of a number of things any of which is a full time job at the moment I do it. I am compensated in the currency of the realm to write and consult. I spent about a quarter of the hours in a day on these activities. Meanwhile, I receive huge psychic reward from grandchildren, family, friends, travel, and the prairie I planted in our front yard. I feel lucky every day for flexibility and fullness of this life I live.

**What is your daily work schedule?**

After a long walk, I eat breakfast and read the newspaper. My goal is to be at my keyboard ready to write by 9 a.m. Email and social media shut off. Door closed. Plenty of coffee at hand. I can be productive writing until noon or 1 p.m. In the afternoon, I follow one of Arthur Miller's writing commandments: "When you can't create, you can work." Afternoons include marketing activities like writing blogs, contacting media, networking. And doing the laundry.

**What is the best writing advice you've ever gotten?**

I've been blessed to learn from many wise writers and teachers. Five bits of wisdom rose to the top a while ago and I captured them on my blog. The piece most relevant at the moment is "Apply Butt Glue." Most books don't get written because the writer didn't commit to being at the keyboard to do the hard work of writing – one word, one sentence, one paragraph, one scene, one chapter at a time. My experience has been that if I stay at the keyboard, something will get written. Maybe not what I thought when I sat down, but something, and that's good enough for me. I am writing the first draft of a new novel and I need to stay at the keyboard – no matter what. Those interested in my other four bits of best writing wisdom, will find it here: http://carolbodensteiner.com/the-best-writing-advice-ever/

## What is the best marketing advice you've ever gotten?

Practice shameless self-promotion. For many authors this is the toughest part, but it's necessary. You can write the best book in the world but no one will buy it if they don't know about it. And who better – or more committed – than the author to carry the good news?

## What has been your best marketing decision so far?

Ready to help readers make a decision. So I worked to do the same. I delayed the publication of Go Away Home for five months while I got advance review copies in the hands of readers. In the first month after publication, I racked up almost 50 reviews, and they kept coming in. That decision was key. The Lake Union Publishing acquisition editor told me the first thing that caught her eye was all the positive reviews. Because of the reviews, she read the novel. When she loved the story, she contacted me about partnering with them. And the rest, as they say, is history. Here's a link to my post about getting reviews: http://carolbodensteiner.com/reviews-matter-heres-how-to-get-them/

**What has been your worst decision as a writer and how did you bounce back?**

Actually, I can't think of a worst decision. I really can't. But the way I think about it, the only bad decision is one you don't learn from, and I learn from everything.

**Let's talk specifically about your deal with Lake Union: how did that happen?**

After Go Away Home had been on the market for six months, an email from an acquisition editor at Lake Union Publishing dropped into my inbox. The editor told me she'd been attracted by the many rave reviews, read the book, loved the story and wanted to talk. I was stunned – and skeptical. I contacted a knowledgeable author friend who said the only reason not to sign on was if I was selling head over heels on my own. I was doing fine by indie standards, but knew it could be better. I joined Lake Union.

**Were you involved in the process of republishing your book?**

Lake Union is very author friendly; they want the author involved every step of the way. The manuscript went through three rounds of editing – developmental, copy, and proofreading. The editors suggested; I rewrote or didn't. It was all my choice. The truth is that I agreed with most of what the editors said. My story is still the same story but it's stronger. I liken the editing process to going to the gym. By working hard at the gym, I'm still me, but I'm a tighter, stronger, better version of me. That's what editing with Lake Union was like.

*Go Away Home* also has a new cover. I really liked my first edition cover, but they felt the cover could do more to convey the historical time period and content of the story. I worked with the cover designer, and together we came up with another good cover.

At the launch, Lake Union told me I could leave marketing in their hands – I could share the news on social media and do local events if I wanted, or not. I've been happy to turn the reins over to them though I can't help but share the news through interviews like this one and with my social media contacts. I'm giddy.

**There's been a lot of talk about the pros and cons of traditional publishing. Is your profit higher now that the book has been republished by Lake Union?**

It's too early to say, since the book just re-launched on July 7. What I can say is that, yes, I made more per copy as an indie publisher. The trade off, I believe, is that Lake Union has the ability to reach far more readers worldwide than I could on my own. While my per copy income will be less, I anticipate I'll more than make that up in quantity. Time will tell.

**What have been the key factors to your success?**

I can point to many factors, starting with:
- My mother. She was the first to encourage me to write, and she never varied in urging, cajoling, nagging me to keep writing. I owe her a great deal. By association, my success is in many ways due to a supportive community of critique partners, workshop leaders and participants, beta readers, and readers in general. I'm grateful to everyone in the village that surrounds my writing.

- Beyond the community, I believe the foremost factor in my success, is that my goal always has been to write the very best stories I can. I'm convinced that's what readers want. I know that's what I want when I pick up a book.
- To accomplish that, I regularly attend workshops to learn and hone my writing craft.
- I invest in the people who can help me publish the very best product: developmental and copy editors, proofreaders, and cover and content designers.
- I learn from everyone and put what I learn into practice.
- I network and pay it forward. Whatever I learn, I happily share, on my blog, one-to-one, or with groups.

**What are your tips for fellow authors who'd like to score a similar deal?**

There's no magic formula, and I recognize that luck played a role in getting a contract with Lake Union. But setting me up for luck was hard work. I wrote the best story I could and got the input of workshops, critique partners, beta readers, and editors to make it better. I hired a professional designer to make the finished book indistinguishable from any book from a traditional publisher. I developed a marketing plan and implemented it. Even with all that, there's no assurance a book will attract a publisher. But you can put yourself in the best position for it to happen.

**What do you think traditional publishers should learn from self-publishers?**

Traditional publishers could learn to be more flexible and nimble. My experience is that Lake Union and the other Amazon Publishing imprints have stepped into this nimble middle ground between indie publishers and the big traditional publishers. They can make decisions and turn a book in a very short period of time. They are partners with their authors. They have embraced digital marketing. Lake Union books can be bought in bricks and mortar stores, but they don't put their energy in getting stacks of books in bookstores.

**What should self-publishers learn from traditional publishers?**

I think many indie authors take short cuts and rush to publication because technology allows it. It's only my opinion, but I think self-publishers should follow the lead of traditional publishers when it comes to investing in editors to make the books the best they can be.

**What do you think the publishing landscape will look like in five years?**

There are really smart people paying attention to that and I'm not one of them. I think the thing that will remain the same in five years is that readers will still want to read good stories.

**Do you think of yourself as an author or as an entrepreneur?**

An author when I'm writing; an entrepreneur when I'm marketing. Because I spent 30 years in the marketing and public relations consulting, the business side runs on autopilot. I'm fortunate in that regard.

**Please share some words of encouragement to authors who are still struggling.**

Keep writing. Give yourself permission to write and enjoy the process. It's most important that you like what you do and are proud of what you write. If you accomplish that, it's all worthwhile.

**Thank you!**

Connect with Carol below:

*Go Away Home*: http://amzn.to/1JKwKpK
*Growing Up Country*: http://amzn.to/KqYbkV
Website: http://www.carolbodensteiner.com
Twitter: @CABodensteiner
Facebook: https://www.facebook.com/CarolBodensteinerAuthor

## Interview with Michelle Weidenbenner

All of her other books were just practice for this one, says Michelle in an interview with a Chicago newspaper. The practice definitely paid off. Michelle is an inspiration for us authors but an even bigger inspiration is Kelly, the girl she wrote the true story about.

I'm honored to have been able to interview Michelle, who is one of us and whose newest release _Fractured Not Broken_ is on top of the charts.

**BIO:** Michelle is an award-winning and best-selling author who lives in Warsaw, Indiana—the orthopedic capital of the world where engineers design hips, knees and shoulders every day.

She's a random girl who writes in random genres and blogs at Random Writing Rants. At home, she's called the 'random subject generator' by her husband of five years.

When she's not writing she's golfing or playing ugly on the tennis court, where she's known as the 'Queen of the Rim Shots'. No joke. It's ugly.

Let's pick Michelle's mind now:

**Why do you write?**

I write because I enjoy telling stories, creating emotion for my readers, and showing them different sides to the same story.

## How long have you been writing?

I decided to take writing classes about 18 years ago, after we adopted our 25-month-old daughter from a Russian orphanage. (Olivia is almost 20 now.) I wanted to be a stay-at-home and work-from-home mom. Initially, I wanted to write for magazines. I thought, how hard can that be?

It was hard. It was difficult to get published. I didn't expect that. Seeing my name in print became an obsession. I went to writers' conferences and met other authors. I took nonfiction and fiction writing courses, and I was hooked. I wanted to create more and more stories. And I wanted to sell my work.

## How long have you been in the self-publishing business?

I published my first novel in July 2013. Two years ago.

## Is writing/publishing your full-time job? If not, what is?

Full time, all the time. But it doesn't feel like a job because I enjoy what I'm doing. Don't get me wrong though, even though I write often, I take time to enjoy life, too. I play tennis and golf and belong to a book club. We read a different book every month and discuss it.

## What is your daily work schedule?

It depends on what I'm working on. If I'm in the throes of writing and creating, I typically arrive at my desk treadmill around 9 a.m. and write until I've met my goal for the day. Sometimes I write a chapter, sometimes more, but during NaNoWriMo my goal is 1,200 words a day. Other days I might edit three chapters. I like to have a weekly goal so I can measure my progress.

Walking on the treadmill while I write helps me feel doubly productive. I can measure how many miles I've walked too. Yes, I write and walk at the same time. Sometimes, especially if I'm editing, clicking my mouse and walking at the same time is a challenge.

## What is the best writing advice you've ever gotten (or read)?

Cec Murphey (*90 Minutes in Heaven*) was my first nonfiction teacher. He said, "Don't beat yourself up if you look back at something you wrote ten years ago and think it was awful. You can only do the best you know how to do right now."

I'm my own worse critic. I never think my writing is good enough. Cec's comment stays with me. I will always want to improve my writing, make it richer. But today I can only use the knowledge I have to write the best I know how to write. Five years from now I might think my writing was terrible, but for today it has to be good enough. (Actually, it might not take five years. I might think it's not good enough tomorrow.)

## What is the best marketing advice you've ever gotten (or read)?

1   To be an author-preneur and treat my writing career as a business, which means having a budget to promo myself, and my books.
2   Finding a really, really good cover artist. (She cost around $300-$350). Let's face it, people judge books by their covers.
3   Hiring an editor and an oops editor to perfect my prose.

## What has been your best marketing decision so far?

I bought Melissa Foster's course *Fostering Success*, which taught me all about pricing, marketing, media releases and cover secrets. Because I bought the course, I was invited to join a closed FB group with other authors. Melissa and other the other authors have been immensely helpful. They're all independently published authors struggling with the same issues, so it's wonderful to help each other along the journey. We learn from one another and encourage each other. Melissa and the team continue to show me marketing ideas that work.

**What has been your worst decision as a writer and how did you bounce back?**

The worse decision was hiring the audio book narrator for my first novel. It was a fiasco which is too long of a story to share here, but I paid half of the cost and discovered the voice I thought I bought wasn't the voice I got. Also, there is SO much work in editing the narration. The narrator expected me to review it all, and it was poorly done. It was the worse money I ever spent. It was easier to abort the project.

**You recently published _Fractured Not Broken_ together with your niece. How was this experience different from publishing your own books?**

This book is nonfiction, so I couldn't make anything up. (Darn!) I have a vivid imagination, so I love to make up stuff. I had to wait to gather the information from Kelly and the other people who were involved in the story. It was different research and a totally new endeavor.

Asking the right questions made all the difference.

Also, Kelly is a quadriplegic. She can't use her legs or arms. Fortunately, she has some use of her left arm, but she types with a mouth stick—very slowly. So all our communication had to be done through voice-to-text or voice-to-email responses. (We live five hours from each other.) There were times when I chuckled at Kelly's responses because it was obvious that the voice activation system hadn't worked. Sentences came out silly and unpredictable.

**In an interview with a Chicago newspaper you said: "I think all my other books were just practice for this one." Can you please elaborate?**

Fiction doesn't always have the same impact on readers as real stories.

I'm often writing several books at one time. So, I have to pay extra attention on which book to focus on, which one will have the most positive impact. Prayer helps me. I ask God to lead my direction, to show me where to spend my time for His will.

I was working on a young adult novel with an editor when I decided to temporarily stop and work with Kelly on her story instead. Her book has a more important message than my YA novel.

Some readers have said Kelly's book will make a great movie. I don't know, but I think it will change lives, and that's important to me. I wonder if God propelled me on a journey to learn how to write so I could tell her story.

**Fractured Not Broken is on top of the charts! Congratulations! How did you achieve this?**

Kelly achieved this. She knows and has inspired so many people! Plus she's a teacher and a speaker, so her reach is far. I built her a Facebook page months before we launched the book and invited people to LIKE the page. Then I started posting little blurbs about our progress. I shared quotes from the book, photos of the people in the book, and questions about who to pitch for endorsements. Within a few weeks of building the FB page, we were interviewed, and an article appeared in her local newspaper. Her FB page continues to grow because we included a link to it at the back of the book. Readers care and want to stay current in Kelly's life.

One reader bought Kelly a pineapple bracelet and wants me to deliver it to her. (The pineapple symbol is a part of the story.) She's never met Kelly, but bought several books to give away as inspirational gifts.

## Do you think of yourself as an author or as an entrepreneur?

I call myself an author-preneur: an author and an entrepreneur. Not only do I need to write a compelling story, but I have to be a savvy business manager and know how to market, sell, and tackle the bookkeeping end of the business, too.

## What have been the key factors to your success?

Stories sell. I think my best-selling book will be Kelly's book because it's a true story, and people seem to migrate to real stories of everyday heroes. I also believe that success (like other things in life, unfortunately) is about whom you know. Kelly has a huge platform of people who are inspired by her teaching, her attitude, and her strength to persevere in the midst of tragedy.

We launched her book a few weeks ago and she's sold more than 2,000 books already. She made the #1 Hot New Release in several categories at Amazon. My phone dings from Facebook comments every hour about how readers love the book, how they are recommending it to everyone. Kelly has been on the radio and television. She's a poised and articulate speaker too, which helps her platform.

Fiction is different. I don't have a huge platform. Yes, I have lots of friends, but spamming friends and family isn't a great way to gain followers. Instead, I rely on BookBub ads to spread the word about my books. Every quarter I feature a different book and offer it for a discount. I've sold over 3,000 books each time I've placed an ad with them. The books sell well after the sale too, because the sale places the book in a higher-ranking status; thus it gains more visibility.

Also, my creative marketing has helped a ton! I sent *Cache a Predator*, my geocaching mystery to geocachers all over the U.S. and Canada to place as a trackable in geocaching sites. It was hours of work to mail the book to fifty readers/cachers, but well worth the time and money. This book sells four times as much as my other fiction because it has more visibility. Geocachers share it at events. They talk about it and recommend it to other avid cachers. Writers have to find creative ways to get in front of readers and make fans. This worked for me.

**What do you think traditional publishers should learn from self-publishers?**

Self-published best-selling authors learned how to sell their books and how to market them by relating to their fans, their audience. They engage in conversations, real human chats at Twitter or FB. They care. They mingle. They aren't afraid to show their human side.

How often do you find a large publishing house 'relating' on a personal level with readers? They're too formal. They need to be more human, show their daily lives, and share their company's journey. The publishing houses need fans — not just reader fans of the books they publish — but fans of their publishing team, the people and face and lives behind their work. They need a 'company' personality that readers love and care about.

## What should self-publishers learn from traditional publishers?

The large traditional publishing houses have more creative talent — people who know how to design a great cover, editors who are better at giving a developmental edit, and editors who know how to edit for grammatical errors and verb tenses, point of view, and typos.

Self-published authors need to take time to learn from their expertise and not be in a hurry to launch their product. More time needs to be spent on editing their book and ensuring that their covers sell. Self-published authors need to establish a budget for their books. In any business, you have to invest money to make money.

**What do you think the publishing landscape will look like in five years?**

Great question! One thing is certain — it won't be the same. It's changed immensely in the last five years, and I anticipate that it will continue, but I love change. I enjoy watching movers and shakers (like you, Alinka), learn how to mix up the industry.

The paradigm shift began a few years ago. Writers were frustrated with the rudeness of the traditional publishing industry — they had to wait months to find an agent, then they waited months to find a publisher. Agents didn't call them back. Publishers rejected their work, but didn't say why. Authors had to rely on someone else to sell their books. Their life-clocks were ticking. They wanted to leave a legacy, and they were anxious to share their work.

But who spent years creating the book? Who knew the book baby? How could they expect someone else to have the same passion for their work?

Many agents are so busy they're poor communicators. They don't have time to write to authors, to send them updates, to send them reasons why they won't accept their work. Some writers are so eager for an agent or publisher they sign deals they shouldn't and find themselves stuck with unsold books in their garage. They give up on their dream and quit writing.

In five years, I think we will see many more self-published authors and less small presses. More authors will learn how to self-publish, but traditional publishers will still be around. Their model will change though. Their book prices will be higher than self-published authors because their overhead will be higher. They will have the manpower to find more creative ways to spread awareness for their books. Academia will continue to support big publishers because overall the quality of writing is more monitored.

But big publishers will find bigger ways to brand themselves. They'll have to if they want to survive.

I love that writers and readers have options though. Don't you?

I think we'll see the birth of a new kind of agent too — one with a team who understands writers, who's designed to help market creative ideas, one who's able to help authors self-publish and teach them how, one who's different from the others. (Hmm, this sounds like something you might like to do, Alinka!)

The writers who become successful bestsellers will know how to market and sell their books and find people like you, Alinka, who will show them how.

**Please share some words of encouragement to authors who are still struggling.**

You can do this on your own! My mother taught me to believe in myself. Keep your eyes on the prize. What is your goal? Believe in yourself.

If you want something bad enough, you will work to attain your goal; you will find the knowledge that will give you the power to exceed. There is free information on the web that can show you how to do write, edit, market and sell your books. Surround yourself with successful people who are helpful, encouraging, and positive. Read books and ask yourself why you liked them, what you would have done differently.

And above all else, never give up. This is your dream. Follow it.

**Thank you!**

**Connect with Michelle below:**

Blog: http://www.randomwritingrants.com

Author page at Amazon: http://
www.amazon.com/Michelle-Weidenbenner/e/
B00E21RMNG/ref=dp_byline_cont_ebooks_1

## Interview with Dennis Thompson

I am delighted to present Dennis Thompson - an author/illustrator who found unique ways of funding and selling his books.

I persuaded Dennis to share his secrets, which he does below, but first let me present him to you properly:

**BIO:** Dennis Thompson is an author and illustrator. His book *The Tale of the Greedy Fish* was published with Kickstarter funding in 2014. The Kickstarter project was funded 151 percent and raised over £4,000.
Dennis helps others to prepare and run crowdfunding projects through his successful crowdfunding blog www.thegreedyfish.net where he publishes free articles regularly as well as promoting current crowdfunding projects.

Dennis sells his books via school visits while teaching children how the book was created, from scribbles and scanning paper, to coloring and compiling the pages on computers.

There are regular updates and special offers on the official website: www.thegreedyfish.co.uk

**You've had great success in crowdfunding your children's book *The Tale of the Greedy***

*Fish* on Kickstarter and you are successfully selling it via school visits. Let's talk about this but first, some background questions:

## Why do you write?

I'm really not sure! I guess like any writer I feel that I have thoughts and ideas I want to share with the world. Whether the world will show any interest is another matter of course. I find myself coming up with ideas almost every day, and writing is a good way to release them from inside my head and driving me crazy. Once they are on paper, or most of the time on a screen, it's easier to judge them and decide whether they are worth pursuing or strike off as a bad idea.

## How long have you been writing?

Ever since I was a child I would write, not anything lengthy, but I always enjoyed poetry and rhymes. This obviously manifests itself in *The Tale of the Greedy Fish*. I have always been a little scared of word counts, so anything I'm writing tends to be quite succinct and to the point.

## How long have you been in the self-publishing business?

Since I self-published *Greedy Fish* in 2014 - it was quite daunting at first as far as ISBN numbers and setting the book up for print, but there's lots of help and advice out there from people like yourself. It's not too hard to find answers to any questions with the help of the internet.

**Is writing/publishing your full-time job? If not, what is?**

I work in a stonemason's office 9-5 Monday to Friday ordering memorials for funeral directors and crematoria. A bit different to making kids books, but they are kind enough to allow me time to visit local schools to promote child literacy through book readings.

**What is your daily work schedule?**

Rarely, if I am up early (and before my three-year-old Heidi is up), I may arrange a little promotion for either my book or blog, then head off to my regular work to start at 9 a.m. Once home in the evening and Heidi has had her dinner, had a bath and a story I can do some 'Author' work from around 8 p.m.! I try to learn as much as I can from YouTube and sites like lynda.com during my lunch breaks and some evenings. I don't have a rigid schedule for any writing and illustrating at present, but I do plan on structuring my time better in the future so I am working on one thing at a time instead of twenty.

**What is the best writing advice you've ever gotten (or read)?**

Perhaps to be prepared for lots of rejection letters. We all think our work is fantastic, but agents and publishers have huge amounts of this 'fantastic' work landing on their desks daily in varying degrees of fantastic-ness. The first few letters were heart breaking. To put all that work into a project to be told 'this does not fit in with our current portfolio' or similar was hard to deal with at first. If you really believe in your work, and you trust the judgment of others that like your work, then self-publishing may be something to consider. Unless you are really lucky or write something genuinely groundbreaking, it's a much more assured way of your book appearing on a shelf somewhere, even if it's just your own shelf.

**What is the best marketing advice you've ever gotten (or read)?**

I have some advice that I have realized myself along my own journey, and that is to give at least some of your work away for free as much as you can. If you can give away electronic copies of your work, it costs nothing, or in my case use the crowdfunding money so it doesn't cost you to give away a physical product. Everyone loves a freebie, and if your work is good, you will get interest from your book being out there. Then when it comes to selling signed copies, or a new edition in the future, people will already hopefully have heard of your book and be willing to support it.

**What has been your best marketing decision so far?**

I have started playing with Google AdWords and Google Analytics - only at a very basic level, and I have started to notice which searches people are using to find my book online, and on which devices (mobile phones/ desktops). I am not sure if paying AdWords is going to prove worthwhile yet, but I can cancel that at anytime and even if I just end up paying about £30 for the first month it has given me some really useful information that I can use to update my website and make it more visible in the future.

**Now let's talk about your Kickstarter campaign. Why did you decide to crowdfund your book?**

I made my book *The Tale of the Greedy Fish* for my daughter Heidi's first birthday as something she could keep forever. I thought initially it would just be an electronic book as I could not afford to get just one copy printed. A friend told about Kickstarter.com, a crowdfunding website, and I started converting my pages into a printable format. I aimed to get funding for 1,000 books which meant I could get them at a reasonable price per unit. I managed to reach 151 percent of my target which meant I could afford 2,000! It still cost me a bit in the end with deliveries, ISBNs etc., but I got the copy for Heidi, and thousands of other children are now enjoying the book too.

**What were the main challenges of your crowdfunding campaign and how did you overcome them?**

My main challenge was not having a clue what I was doing! I was almost completely unprepared for running a fresh and interesting campaign for 30 days - all the promo work, posters, online adverts and sharing to social media networks meant I was up early each morning, and up late every night posting and preparing things every single day. This is one of the reasons I have started my successful crowdfunding blog - to help others prepare better from all I have learned in my own experience of crowdfunding.

**What should authors know/do before they start a crowdfunding campaign?**

Be prepared! You really have to be visible to everyone you possibly can before the project starts as far ahead as possible, and anything you can do to get each days promotion ready before you start will make the job a lot easier. Decide what you will do, where and what you will post on each and every day the project is running. Plan interviews and any press coverage well beforehand - not on the fly like I did!

## Any other advice on crowdfunding for authors?

Learn all you can from other crowdfunders, read my blog, and get involved funding some projects yourself so you can see how others communicate with funders and promote their projects from start to finish. Take note of the good and bad to tailor your own to be the best it can be.

## Now let's talk about school visits. How did you get involved in these?

I was actually asked by one of the original funders if I would visit a school and present a copy of the book to their grandson. I did this, and got a great response from donating 20 or so copies to the school. I was then asked by others to visit their children's schools as well. It was never planned, but has become one of the most enjoyable parts of the whole experience.

## How can an author get an invitation to a school?

I often get asked directly by the schools, but also send copies of my book offering a visit. As simple as that! The only thing you may need is public liability insurance just in case of an accident - dropping a box of books on a child's foot could really spoil the party.

## What do you do during a school visit?

To begin with I stand up nervously as the teachers introduce me to the class or assembly! I always get a little stage fright. But once I start reading the book and seeing the kids enjoying it I relax and enjoy it enormously myself. Afterwards all the children get a chance to ask me questions about the book (and some totally unrelated questions about their pets and video games), I sign copies of the books for anyone that might like one, and then I head back to work.

## Do you get paid?

I never take any money for the visits, and I always give a free copy to the school for their library. Lots of the schools I visit do not have the funds for many new books, so the free copies are always welcome. My only income is through book sales and as long as the cost of the book printing is covered then I can carry on in this way. Children and parents get a bargain book, and hopefully I might inspire a few future authors and artists.

**How many books do you sell at school visits? Do you offer discounts?**

I offer signed copies of my book as discounted as I can afford to anyone in schools that would like one after the readings, which covers the cost of the printing them. I also sell the books on amazon.co.uk and through my website which occasionally has some kind of discount available.

**Any tips for authors going on a school visit?**

Have fun! The kids love to join in and heckle and laugh, so give them every opportunity to do so. These kids are your potential future audience, so any encouragement to get children reading will only do good for authors everywhere.

**What else would you like to achieve as an author?**

I have a number of other projects I am working on, so there may be another illustrated children's book (not about a fish!), and if I ever get the time I have an adult novel I have been preparing all my life - it would be nice to get that out finally. I would love to be published and be a 'paid' author, but if I can encourage a few children to read along the way doing what I am doing now then I will be happy with that.

## Interview with Chandler Bolt

Entrepreneur of the Year and best-selling author Chandler Bolt graciously accepted my invitation to this interview despite his tight schedule.

He not only replies to all my questions but also provides us with a free video training session which reveals how to write, publish, and market your book - even if you don't have time, writing skills, or a book idea.

**BIO:** Chandler was bit by the entrepreneurial bug at an early age when he saw that he could make a lot more money working for himself. While his friends were off searching for jobs, he was out starting businesses.

He began early (aged 11) by selling his personal snacks at scout camp and, by the age of 17 he had hired his friends to help him operate his landscaping business that earned him $10,000 for college. All in all, by the age of 20 he had turned over $320,000 in businesses he had started.

During this time, he taught other college students how to run their own successful businesses and received the Entrepreneur of the Year award from Young Entrepreneurs Across America.

Chandler now speaks to students across the country teaching them the lessons he's learned as a young entrepreneur and encouraging them to take the entrepreneurial leap. He is also the founder of Self-Publishing School.

Let's pick Chandler's mind now:

**Why do you write?**

I write because it's my way to reach the masses. So I can distill my knowledge down once and reach a mass audience forever. It's timeless and it'll live on forever.

**How long have you been writing?**

I started out a really, really bad writer and I've actually - I was a C English student and I just sucked at writing and I hated it. Then I wrote my first book and everything kind of changed from there. So I've learned to love writing and I've learned to be good at it but I've only been doing it for the last three or four years.

**How long have you been in the self-publishing business?**

The same amount of time. I wrote and published my first book about three years ago and I've done five books since then.

**Is writing publishing your full-time job, if not, what is?**

Yes it is, I run <u>Self-Publishing School</u>. That's where I teach other people how to write, market, and publish their first book in 90 days or less, and it's mostly geared towards nonfiction. So I'm either working on books or I'm helping other people write, market, and publish their books through my program.

**What's your daily work schedule?**

I get up at 6:00 every morning. I have a morning routine that includes reading, some journaling, exercise, all that, and then I always do my highest leverage work - whether that be writing or that be high leverage activity - first thing in the morning. So my mornings are always sacred. And then Monday, Wednesday, Friday are what I call buffer days. So that's where I have most of my meetings, podcast interviews, things like that. But then Tuesday and Thursday are my focus days. So that's where I really get a lot done on those days.

**What's the best writing advice you've ever gotten or read?**

That is my crappy book is better than the book you ain't got, which is obviously very not correct grammar. But it's so true. A finished book is better than someone who's making fun of you that doesn't have a book written at all. The best marketing advice I've ever gotten is shotgun versus rifle approach. Most people approach marketing a book like shooting a shotgun, where they just spray everywhere and hope that something hits. But I prefer to use the rifle method and focus in on just what works.

**What's been your best marketing decision so far?**

It's honestly been to publish my first book, and to build an email list right after that.

**What's been your worst decision as a writer and how did you bounce back?**

Worst decision as a writer would probably be not doing an outline. I do it now, but I used to hear the advice of doing an outline to begin with and I said, "Oh, that's stupid." Then I just started writing. But once I really started getting into writing books I realized that the outline is everything. If you do the outline it makes all of your work easier, so it's very important to do that.

**What do you think of yourself as an author and entrepreneur?**

I think I'm a decent author, and that's something I'm getting better at. I think I'm probably a better entrepreneur. I really love growing things. I've been able to build Self-Publishing School really quickly and at a young age, and I'd say I'm a pretty skilled entrepreneur. But both are things that I'm learning.

**What would be the key factors to your success?**

I'd say my work ethic number one. I work harder than pretty much anyone, and then I would say my discipline. And so that's discipline to put in the work day in and day out, even when it's not easy, and even when it's not something I want to do, or when I'm having a rough day. I have the discipline to stick through and to push past that.

**What do I think traditional publishers should learn from self-publishers?**

How to actually market and sell books. I think that traditional publishers are very dated and they've learned how to retain power of a couple of key things, but I think traditional publishers can learn pretty much everything from self-publishers. Because I think traditional publishers suck. They do a very poor job of marketing. In fact, they do zero marketing and everyone who's published a book knows that. So I think they could learn how to market and actually sell books.

**What should self-publishers learn from traditional publishers?**

I'd say how to get better distribution and how to do a big scale launch. So the distribution really helps with that, but what a lot of self-publishers need to learn is the fundamentals behind that. So the build up, the PR, the traveling. The different things that happen not necessarily because of publishers but as a by-product of releasing a published book. So that's something that they could learn.

**What is a Self-Publishing Success Summit and how did it start?**

The Self-Publishing Success Summit was an online event taught by people who had written or published a book. And it was all about how to help people write, market, and publish their first book. And how to build a brand, business, or following through a book taught by people who have done it. There were tons of experts in all different industries. Not self-publishing gurus, but people who built their business brand or following through a book and they were teaching the best stuff that they learned in the summit.

**What is Self-Publishing School?**

Self-Publishing School is an online training program where we teach people to write, market, and publish their first book, and use it to build their business brand or following. It's mostly geared toward non fiction but we also have a lot of fiction writers as well. And in Self-Publishing School it's the training program but it's also the community and it's a really supportive group of people who help people write, market, publish their first book in 90 days or less.

**How did it start?**

It all started when I did my first book and I launched my first book and I quickly made $6,000 in the first month off my first book, and then it continued to cash flow $4,000 to $6,000 a month. Then I did another book, and then I helped a friend do a book, and I felt like a broken record because I kept having the same conversation over and over and over again about books helping people. Then finally so many people asked about it I said, "Okay, this is something I should focus on, and this is something I'm going to do."

**Please share some student success stories.**

I'd say the success stories from our program are insane. Our success rate is through the roof, and it's better than any other program I've ever heard of. And the common thing that we get from our students is it's the first online program that they bought that's actually given them a tangible result. So it's not uncommon for students to graduate the program and obviously have a book - a tangible book. Something that they can be proud of. Something that can give them confidence, can give them success, and open up other opportunities. But also it's very common for students to have either thousands a month in passive income. It opens up the door for speaking gigs. It opens up for coaching, for running their business. Our big thing though is it's about what the book can do for you not just about the book itself. Where people get caught up is in the trap of how much passive income can I make immediately. We tend to focus more on what the book opens up.

Just the other day, we had one of our students that just got booked for a $3,000 speaking gig, their first ever speaking gig, all because of their book. Other students make $3,000 to $4,000 a month in passive income. Other students have made $12,000, $15,000, $17,000 off of clients that have brought in from their books. There are all kinds of success stories in different ways.

**Why should authors consider signing up for Self-Publishing School?**

If you've always thought about writing a book but you've never done it, I'd say our course is a great fit for you. If you're an author that's struggling to sell books and you want to learn how to do this the right way and actually sell books, I'd say that self-publishing school can be a good fit for you too. We definitely know what we're doing when it comes to the marketing.

**What are things authors will learn in SPS?**

They'll learn how to write, and market, and publish their first book. It's the A to Z on the whole process. We teach some in-depth marketing. We teach how to get an editor. We teach how to write the book, how to write it well, how to format it, how to publish it. All the logistics, everything you need to know start to finish. But we're also very conscious to limit the amount of material in there, so that it doesn't cause overwhelm.

**When can authors enroll?**

You'll just have to check out and look out for our next enrollment period.

**What do you think the publishing landscape will look like in five years?**

Our goal with self-publishing school is to put the publishers out of business. So I think that the publishers will be out of business in five years, and self-publishing will not only be a viable option, but it will be the best option.

You'll see a lot more independent publishers, a lot of people will be self-publishing books.

**Please share some words of encouragement for other authors who are still struggling.**

I would say that just get in there and do it. Your first book isn't going to be your best book. Just get something to the finish line. Doesn't mean it has to be crappy work. I definitely don't mean that. But just get in there. Get that rough draft finished. Especially if it's your first book, that's really going to help. And once you get that finished you'll be able to really run with it.

**Thank you!**

## Interview with Mark Dawson

Best-selling author Mark Dawson has become the go-to person when it comes to using paid traffic to add readers to your mailing list and boost the sales of your books. His course, *Facebook Ads for Authors*, caused quite a stir when it was launched for the first time in June this year. He enrolled 450 indie authors, including some of the biggest in the world, and provided them with high quality online teaching that showed them exactly how to use Facebook to give their writing careers a big boost. I've been in touch with Mark since then.

I went through his course and I can say one thing with absolute confidence: this is the best produced, most focused, most actionable course available for authors and writers who want to leverage the world's most powerful social network to take their publishing careers to the next level.

Thanks to Mark's course, I'd like to welcome 357 new authors (who have subscribed within the last seven days). You know that you're here because of my Facebook ads - I was following Mark's lessons!

And now, with no further ado, let me present...DRUMROLL...Mark Dawson who has honored us with a fantastic interview!

**BIO:** Mark Dawson has worked as a lawyer and currently works in the London film industry. His first books, *The Art of Falling Apart* and *Subpoena Colada* have been published in multiple languages.

He is currently writing three series.

The John Milton series features a disgruntled assassin who aims to help people to make amends for the things that he has done.

The Beatrix Rose series features the headlong fight for justice of a wronged mother - who happens to be an assassin - against the six names on her kill list.

Soho Noir is set in the West End of London between 1940 and 1970. The first book in the series, *The Black Mile*, deals with the (real life but little known) serial killer who operated in the area during the Blitz. *The Imposter* traces the journey of a criminal family through the period; it has been compared to The Sopranos in austerity London.

Mark lives in Wiltshire, England, with his family.

**Mark, why do you write?**

Because I have no choice in the matter. It's what I love to do, and I'd do it even if there were no prospect of ever selling another book.

**How long have you been writing?**

Since I was 13 or 14.

**How long have you been in the self-publishing business?**

Since 2012/2013.

**Is writing/publishing your full-time job? If not, what is?**

This is the full-time job now.

**What is your daily work schedule?**

I get up at 6 and get my children ready for the day. Then, after delivering them to their nursery, I start work. I'll usually write from 8.30 until around 12.30, then I'll change venues and take care of business tasks. That can take a couple of hours these days. Once that's done, I'll try and write for another hour or two. I'll usually finish working at 5.30.

**What is the best writing advice you've ever received (or read)?**

Writers write. You can't call yourself a writer unless you get down and start doing it. And, also, you should write what you want to write (and read, perhaps) rather than what you think the market wants. The market changes its mind.

**What is the best marketing advice you've ever gotten (or read)?**

You have to treat it as a business. That means you have to treat it professionally, and you have to be prepared to invest time and money into making it work. Success will not fall in your lap – that is a guarantee.

**What has been your best marketing decision so far?**

Learning how to use Facebook ads. I was doing very well before I started to advertise; now I am doing extremely well.

**What has been your worst decision as a writer and how did you bounce back?**

I was a bit slow in getting my mailing list up and running; I lost time in making progress, but that's a problem that is easily fixed. Start the list!

**You've had great success with Facebook ads - how did Facebook ads help grow your business?**

They have helped me to find new readers with subscription campaigns and sell books, too. I'm on track to spending around $150,000 this year in advertising, but the return is likely to be twice that. You don't have to start with a massive budget, though. When I started experimenting, I did it on $5 a day and then reinvested the profits. It took off from that point and hasn't stopped yet.

**Many authors fail at using Facebook ads to grow their business - what are they doing wrong?**

They thinking hitting 'boost' is how to advertise on Facebook. It isn't. Others ignore advice from other authors who are having success and plough on regardless. When I started, there were no writers explaining what you needed to do, so I taught myself through podcasts and articles from other industries that were a little ahead of us.

**Can you share some best practices on how to make FB ads work?**

You have to test obsessively. You are unlikely to stumble upon the best combination of ad image, copy and targeting immediately. One well-known author I have taught ran through 38 different iterations until he found one that worked. And now that one is returning his investment at 100 percent. Worth the effort.

**Do you think of yourself as an author or as an entrepreneur?**

Both. You need to be able to switch hats at, well, the drop of a hat.

**What have been the key factors to your success?**

First of all, I know my strengths and weaknesses. I am a very good writer. I am not a very good cover designer. I am prepared to pay skilled designers and editors to do the things that I can't do. I'm tenacious, thirsty to learn and prepared to make mistakes if that means my knowledge is improved. I am determined to make it work. And I know how to turn readers into fans into raving fans and then into friends. If you do that, adding them one at a time, you can make a very good living for yourself. And it's easy to do: just be friendly and normal. Good things will happen.

**What do you think traditional publishers should learn from self-publishers?**

How to publish books in the 21st century. Pricing. How to attract fans and keep them happy.

**What should self-publishers learn from traditional publishers?**

Take editing and cover design seriously.

**What do you think the publishing landscape will look like in five years?**

The distinction between indie and traditional publishing will have blurred even more to the point where it is indistinguishable. Amazon will be challenged more by Apple and Google but will still be dominant.

**Please share some words of encouragement to authors who are still struggling.**

Write! If you don't enjoy it, maybe it's not for you. But if you do, and you are prepared to work hard, you can do amazing things and change your life.

**Thank you, Mark!**

## YOU'RE NOT ALONE

I know this was A LOT to process, and you're a hero if you got to the end of this book!

If you have a visual type of memory, you will enjoy the one-page diagram I prepared for you. It covers the contents of this book on only one page. Download it here: http://alinkarutkowska.com/his8b/

But it's really just the basics. There's much more to know and many of the topics we've covered have a significant depth to them, which is impossible to explain in detail in a book like this.

That's why I created Author Remake: an actionable step-by-step video coaching system in which I guide you through the 4 Ps in a way that allows you to focus on the 20% of book marketing efforts that bring 80% of results.

Get the first seven video lessons for free at authorremake.com.

# FREE VIDEO TRAINING

Get the step-by-step system I use to sell books by the truckload: authorremake.com

Go to authorremake.com — I'll see you on the inside!

# REVIEW REQUEST

Do as I say, not as I do. Just kidding. In this book I recommend that you ask your readers to post a review of your book.

So, in order to be completely compliant with what I preach, here's my request:

*If you enjoyed this book,*
*And learnt from it too,*
*Why not then go online*
*to write a sweet review!*

**Thank you!**

Made in the USA
Columbia, SC
19 January 2018

87820859R00100